BEYOND CATASTROPHE
The Rabbis' Reading of Isaiah's Vision

SOUTH FLORIDA STUDIES IN THE HISTORY OF JUDAISM

Edited by
Jacob Neusner
William Scott Green, James Strange
Darrell J. Fasching, Sara Mandell

Number 131
BEYOND CATASTROPHE
The Rabbis' Reading of Isaiah's Vision

by
Jacob Neusner

BEYOND CATASTROPHE

The Rabbis' Reading of Isaiah's Vision

ISRAELITE MESSIAH-PROPHECIES IN FORMATIVE JUDAISM

An Anthology of Pesiqta deRab Kahana
for the Seven Sabbaths after the Ninth of Ab

by

Jacob Neusner

Scholars Press
Atlanta, Georgia

BEYOND CATASTROPHE
The Rabbis' Reading of Isaiah's Vision

BM
615
.P4713
1996

by
Jacob Neusner

©1996
University of South Florida

Publication of this book was made possible by a grant from the Tisch Family Foundation, New York City. The University of South Florida acknowledges with thanks this important support for its scholarly projects.

Library of Congress Cataloging in Publication Data
Pesikta de-Rav Kahana XVI–XXII. English
    Beyond catastrophe : the Rabbis' reading of Isaiah's vision :
Israelite messiah-prophecies in formative Judaism : an anthology of
Pesiqta deRab Kahana for the seven sabbaths after the Ninth of Ab /
by Jacob Neusner.
        p.   cm. — (South Florida studies in the history of Judaism ;
no. 131)
    ISBN 0-7885-0214-X (alk. paper)
    1. Messiah—Judaism. 2. Holocaust (Jewish theology) 3. Bible.
O.T. Isaiah XL–LXI—Criticism, interpretation, etc. 4. Pesikta de-
Rav Kahana XVI–XXII—Criticism, interpretation, etc. I. Neusner,
Jacob, 1932–   . II. Title. III. Series: South Florida studies in
the history of Judaism ; 131.
BM615.P4713 1996
296.1'4—dc20   95-51832
                                                 CIP

Printed in the United States of America
on acid-free paper

TABLE OF CONTENTS

Preface

Holy Israel, the people that God called into being at Sinai and sanctifies with the Torah and commandments, through all time always responds to catastrophe with the renewed confidence of God's love and restored faith in God's promises that the figure of the Messiah embodies. In the time of Holocaust that response now requires renewal. In these pages I show how in the formative age of the history of Judaism, the hope for the coming of the Messiah defined Israel's response to calamity and catastrophe. That demonstration of how we of holy Israel have been taught to respond to the terror of history takes on urgency because today this-worldly Israel has chosen another way, a different mode of response, one that I believe should stand in the context of, and in comparison with, the response called forth by the faith of the Torah. Here, in these pages, I set forth the Torah's — that is, Judaism's — counterpart to today's Holocaust museums and monuments.

This anthology draws upon the resources of the oral part of the Torah to take up the acutely critical issue of contemporary Judaism, which is, the proper mode of response to the Holocaust. Here I show how our sages of blessed memory determined to take account of historical calamity. By reading how sages formulated the synagogue lections for the Sabbaths following the commemoration of catastrophe on the ninth of Ab, we see the way in which they transformed the crisis of faith precipitated by the encounter with evil into the occasion for renewal and regeneration nourished by Israel's prophets in particular. Here is the point at which the coming of the Messiah imposes upon catastrophe God's perspective and God's message: enduring love, renewed hope, embodied in the grace of the Messiah's advent. The Messiah for whom Israel waits bears love, and only love, for Israel in the very setting of the Torah that announces the Messiah's coming. Seen in the context of contemporary faith, turning toward the acute concern in both Judaic and Christian religious communities with how to think about the Holocaust, this anthology means to give voice to Israel's prophets and sages and their message of transformation.

To spell out why I conceive that the synagogue lections concerning the coming of the Messiah that are taken up in these pages form an alternative to the building of Holocaust memorials as the medium of response to the calamity of our century, let me begin with not the early centuries of the Common Era, which speak in these pages, but with our own time. The one message drew upon hope to speak of the coming of the Messiah as God's consolation and the mark of God's enduring love, the other underscores the despair catastrophe itself conveys. To make this point specific: the glory of Israel, the Jewish people, shines in the renewal of life that has taken place from 1945. God's first love, Israel, the holy people, offered the world the lesson of resurrection by an act of will: we chose not to die. The shame of that same, this-worldly Israel, lies in the acts of commemoration that have committed forgetfulness against the Torah by recalling everything that took place but forgetting the context of all events, which is set forth by God in the Torah. The act of memorialization set forth a profound statement on what was to be forgotten, which out of the context of the sacred history of holy Israel is, the entire existence of holy Israel itself, before, during, and after those uniquely terrible events. But the Holocaust out of the context of the Torah, which is to say in its secular category, Judaism, bears only a negative message. The Holocaust in the setting of the Torah takes on the dimensions of not only terror but grandeur, not only calamity but the testament of faith and hope, that every calamity in Israel's long and often sad history must bear. The Holocaust viewed outside of the faith of the Torah of Israel affirmed nothing and meant nothing beyond a mere ethnic, demographic disaster — to be recovered from, but not to be turned into an occasion for regeneration and inner rebirth: "Though he slay me, yet will I trust in him."

A mark of the failure of religious faith in the Torah, the ethnicization of the Holocaust, the massive silence enveloping the Torah's perspectives — these have deprived the generations from 1945 of all nourishment, such that the Torah affords by reason of its sacred perspective upon humanity. Job and Jeremiah, wisdom and prophecy — in both holy Israel has found transforming hope in the darkest days of historical crisis. But in our generation wisdom and prophecy have found themselves dismissed, given no opportunity to make their statement. Rabbinic literature, with its profound reflection on Israel's fate, rarely gained its voice and delivered its statement. Israel, the Jewish people, quite properly reaffirmed its worldly life and rebuilt and renewed itself. Israel, the holy people, fell silent. So the State of Israel, formed in the aftermath of the calamity in Europe, and the renewal of Judaism in a strong and united Jewish community in the USA and throughout the free world, even the rebirth of Jewry in the long-silent realm of atheistic Communism — these miracles of the human spirit, which in another age would have attested to God's comfort and God's judgment, in our own day have gained a merely this-worldly resonance. Nation reborn and rebuilt, the ethnic group in the West reconstituted have attested only to the might of Israel, the Jewish people, but not to the miracle of God. And yet, to any reasonable person of religious sensibility, the capacity of mortally-wounded Israel, the Jewish people, to accomplish the great deeds of the past half-century surely bears a religious message about God's working among us.

People have accomplished wonders. Is God not to be invoked? The survivors emerged and reaffirmed the very thing the enemy proposed to extirpate: I will not die but live. But only few then completed the imperative: ...and declare the works of the Lord. Remembering what happened then took a quite unique form: the Torah for the first time in the history of Judaism and of the Jewish people found no hearing. The greatest calamity in the history of the Jewish people did not provoke wide and deep reflection on lessons and messages that the Torah in both its media, written and oral, and all of its diverse and complex statements, was meant to set forth. The modes of memory remained wholly secular, testament to the unfaith of the most faithful people of recorded time. New modes of commemoration replaced the received ones, those of the Torah, and history was ignored, only to rehearsed, now with no compelling script at all.

In reflecting and remembering the catastrophe of 1933-1945 (5700-5705 by the calendar of Judaism), most of Israel, the Jewish people, lost sight of itself as Israel, the holy people. Memorials to the Holocaust take shape as though in recorded time we have learned nothing but forgotten everything. Special days designated to the mourning of the recent past ignored the long and enduring record of Israel's suffering, commemorated on the ninth of Ab (ordinarily: the lunar month that falls in late July or early August): the destruction of the first Temple in 586 B.C.E.(=B.C.), the destruction of the second Temple in 70 C.E. (=A.D.), the expulsion of the Jews from Spain in 1492, and countless calamities, before and since, all of them remembered and mourned, but also transformed into occasion of renewal, through time. Properly insisting that, in the secular context, the Holocaust represented a moment unique in humanity's history, Israel the Jewish people drew the improper conclusion that nothing, then, is to be learned from historical record, no lesson to be derived from the heritage of the past. That is why in place of the ninth of Ab, a new commemorative occasion had to be fabricated, the State of Israel designating the Holocaust memorial day in the very context of its own Independence Day. That is why, in place of the religious rites of memory yielding regeneration — God brings comfort and loves Israel — secular rituals of memory lacking all constructive meaning take over. Holocaust museums today replace holy places.

These museums cast a dark shadow over faith. For holy Israel builds its cathedrals in time, not in space, so Abraham J. Heschel observed, and despite the contrary appearance of the moment, over time holy places in a single location, the Land of Israel, always give way to the enduring and sustaining and ubiquitous moments of sanctification. That fact governs not only the Sabbath or Passover of the Day of Atonement but also the ninth of Ab — and then also, the six Sabbaths that come in sequence thereafter. The ninth of Ab, commemorating all calamity and catastrophe, defines the occasion, in the liturgy of the synagogue, for the celebration of God's love, the recognition of God's yearning for Israel and enduring, unconditional grace, for holy Israel. The wisdom of the sages who framed the liturgy of the synagogue comes to expression in the selection of the prophetic lections to follow the intense mourning of the ninth of Ab, lections that, over the next six weeks, proclaim that other side of history of which the Torah, and the Torah alone, takes the measure. If attached to every Holocaust Museum were a synagogue and study place, in which constant study of the Torah, prayer, and recitation of Psalms took place, then we should have in a locative framework the counterpart to the utopian liturgical commemoration of Israel's calamity in the very context of God's enduring concern for Israel. The fact that not a single Holocaust Museum in the entire world makes provision for regular, on-going activities of prayer, Torah-study, and recitation of God's praise in the Psalms, testifies to the deeply anti-Judaic character of our generation's response to its time of trial — the trial, I mean, of not mass murder but surviving mass murder.

To set forth that other Israel, holy Israel, and its way of addressing calamity, not merely coping with memory by memorialization but drawing renewal from events through fresh learning in the Torah, I set forth in this anthology a systematic reading of the prophetic passages that follow the ninth of Ab in the synagogue lections. In this way I place on display that other way, the way of faith and hope and regeneration, that the Torah opens up to the pilgrim people in its passage through time. Here are the lessons to be received when memory has come to the surface, and the disheartening events of suffering and death have formed consciousness: this too we remember, along with suffering, and these things too we call to mind, along with doubt and despair.

Here is how our sages of blessed memory — the rabbis of the Talmud and Midrash that record in writing the originally oral part of the Torah of Sinai — teach Israel to respond to the memories invoked by the ninth of Ab. The prophetic lections for the six Sabbaths after the ninth of Ab are spelled out in a systematic way to yield a single message. It is one that concerns the Messiah, who stands for God's loyalty to, and love for, holy Israel, including all who throughout recorded time have joined holy Israel at Sinai with the affirmation, "we shall do and we shall obey," in accepting the Torah of the one and only God of all creation. In asking contemporaries to reconsider how our sages took up the challenge of catastrophe, in insisting that here, in these words, we contemplate the authentic "Holocaust museum" that Israel's inner conscience formed in response to the imperative of the living God, I wish to show not only what might have been and what has been but also what should be: the way of faith that Israel's sages have explored for us.

The plan of the book belies its intent and program. In Chapter One I provide an introduction to the substance of matter, the importance of the Messiah-theme at a particular moment in the formative history of Judaism. Then, as is my way, I step aside and ask our sages of blessed memory to speak in their way about their concerns. It is only in these brief, prefatory remarks that I specify why I think it is urgent at just this time and place to pay attention to the sages' words. The opening chapters make the case that when sages raise the subject of the Messiah in the formative age, it is in response to specific historical events, seen as ominous and threatening. That fact forms the bridge I mean to build between the Messiah-theme and the crisis of the Holocaust, and how I propose contemporary holy Israel is to address the Holocaust in the context of the Torah then comes to full expression in the passages of the great, systematic reading of the Messiah-prophecies that I lay out in full.

Chapter One reviews the main results of these works of mine: *The Foundations of Judaism. Method, Teleology, Doctrine*. Philadelphia, 1983-5: Fortress Press. I-III. II. *Messiah in Context. Israel's History and Destiny in Formative Judaism*. Second printing: Lanham, 1988: University Press of America. Studies in Judaism series; *Judaisms and their Messiahs in the beginning of Christianity*. New York, 1987: Cambridge University Press; *Ancient Judaism and Modern Category-Formation. "Judaism," "Midrash," "Messianism," and Canon in the Past Quarter-Century*. Lanham, 1986: University Press of America *Studies in Judaism* Series; and *Rabbinic Judaism. Structure and System*. Minneapolis, 1995: Fortress Press. The translations derive from my *Pesiqta deRab Kahana. An Analytical Translation and Explanation*. I. *1-14*. Atlanta, 1987: Scholars Press for Brown Judaic Studies. My introduction to the document comes from *The Doubleday Anchor Reference Library Introduction to Rabbinic Literature*. N.Y., 1994: Doubleday.

I edited this anthology during my tenure as Canterbury Visiting Fellow at the University of Canterbury in Christchurch, New Zealand. I express my thanks to the many friends and colleagues who made that stay a memorable and happy one, in particular my study-mate and friend from Clare Hall, Cambridge, Dr. David Gunby, Department of English at Canterbury, who originally proposed the visit that proved so felicitous in so many ways. My personal tribute to the the high intellectual standards of the Christian communities of Christchurch, if not the students at Canterbury University — few of whom attended what were very well-attended lectures! — is contained in my addresses prepared for that community and now published as *Judaism after the Death of "the Death of God." The Canterbury Addresses and Other Essays on the Renaissance of Judaism in Contemporary Jewry*. Atlanta, 1994: Scholars Press for South Florida Studies in the History of Judaism. The title of my Canterbury addresses by itself places into context this anthology as well. The time has come, so I maintain, to speak plainly about God in the very center of the life of Israel, God's first love, and at the critical heart of Israel's immediate concern: the secular ethnicization has had its say, now let us hear, once more, from the sacred teachings of the Torah.

I completed work on this little book at home, at the University of South Florida. That is appropriate, for nothing I do takes place outside of the setting of life at the University of South Florida. No one in the academic world enjoys more favorable circumstances for scholarship than I do as Distinguished Research Professor in the Florida State University System. I express my thanks for not only the advantage of a Distinguished Research Professorship in the Florida state university system, which for a scholar must be the best job in the world, but also of a substantial research expense fund, ample research time, and stimulating, straight-forward, and cordial colleagues, many of whom also are cherished friends.

JACOB NEUSNER

CANTERBURY VISITING FELLOW
UNIVERSITY OF CANTERBURY
CHRISTCHURCH, NEW ZEALAND
AND
DISTINGUISHED RESEARCH PROFESSOR OF RELIGIOUS STUDIES
UNIVERSITY OF SOUTH FLORIDA

TAMPA, FLORIDA 33620-5550 U.S.A.

I

Teleology and Eschatology
The Messiah in the Context
of Formative Judaism

I. THE MISHNAH'S TELEOLOGY WITHOUT ESCHATOLOGY

The formative history of Judaism beyond the Hebrew Scriptures of ancient Israel reaches its initial written expression in the Mishnah, a philosophical law code of ca. 200 C.E. What is surprising is that, in that generative writing, the Messiah-theme plays no formidable role. When constructing a systematic account of Judaism — that is, the worldview and way of life for Israel presented in the Mishnah — the philosophers of the Mishnah did not make use of the Messiah-myth in the construction of a teleology for their system.[1] They found it possible to present a statement of goals for their projected life of Israel that was entirely separate from appeals to history and eschatology. Since they certainly knew, and even alluded to, long-standing and widely held convictions on eschatological subjects, beginning with those in Scripture, the framers thereby testified that, knowing the larger repertoire, they made choices different from others before and after them. Their document accurately and ubiquitously expresses these choices, both affirmative and negative.

Now that fact is surprising, for the character of the Israelite Scriptures, with their emphasis upon historical narrative as a mode of theological explanation, leads us to expect all Judaisms to evolve as deeply messianic religions. With all prescribed actions pointed toward the coming of the Messiah at the end of time,

---

[1] This chapter reviews the results of *The Foundations of Judaism. Method, Teleology, Doctrine.* Philadelphia, 1983-5: Fortress Press. I-III. II. *Messiah in Context. Israel's History and Destiny in Formative Judaism.* Second printing: Lanham, 1988: University Press of America. Studies in Judaism series, and *Judaism and Christianity in the Age of Constantine. Issues of the Initial Confrontation.* Chicago, 1987: University of Chicago Press.

and all interest focused upon answering the historical-salvific questions ("how long?"), Judaism from late antiquity to the present day presents no surprises. Its liturgy evokes historical events to prefigure salvation; prayers of petition repeatedly turn to the speedy coming of the Messiah; and the experience of worship invariably leaves the devotee expectant and hopeful. Just as Rabbinic Judaism is a deeply messianic religion, secular extensions of Judaism have commonly proposed secularized versions of the focus upon history and have shown interest in the purpose and denouement of events. Teleology again appears as an eschatology embodied in messianic symbols.

Yet, for a brief moment, the Mishnah presented a kind of Judaism in which history did not define the main framework by which the issue of teleology took a form other than the familiar eschatological one, and in which historical events were absorbed, through their trivialization in taxonomic structures, into an ahistorical system. In the kind of Judaism in this document, Messiahs played a part. But these "anointed men" had no historical role. They undertook a task quite different from that assigned to Jesus by the framers of the Gospels. They were merely a species of priest, falling into one classification rather than another.

The Mishnah finds little of consequence to say about the Messiah as savior of Israel, one particular person at onetime, but manages to set forth its system's teleology without appeal to eschatology in any form. For the Mishnah, "Messiah" is a category of priest or general. The Messiah-theme proved marginal to the system's program. By ca. A.D. 400, by contrast, a system of Judaism emerged in the pages of the Talmud of the Land of Israel, in which the Mishnah as foundation document would be asked to support a structure at best continuous with, but in no way fully defined by the outlines of, the Mishnah itself. Coming at the system from the asymmetrical endpoint, we ask the Mishnah to answer the questions at hand. What of the Messiah? When will he come? To whom, in Israel, will he come? And what must, or can, we do while we wait to hasten his coming? If we now re-frame these questions and divest them of their mythic cloak, we ask about the Mishnah's theory of the history and destiny of Israel and the purpose of the Mishnah's own system in relationship to Israel's present and end: the implicit teleology of the philosophical law at hand.

Answering these questions out of the resources of the Mishnah is not possible. The Mishnah presents no large view of history. It contains no reflection whatever on the nature and meaning of the destruction of the Temple in A.D. 70, an event that surfaces only in connection with some changes in the law explained as resulting from the end of the cult. The Mishnah pays no attention to the matter of the end time. The word "salvation" is rare, "sanctification" commonplace. More strikingly, the framers of the Mishnah are virtually silent on the teleology of the system; they never tell us why we should do what the Mishnah tells us, let alone explain what will happen if we do. Incidents in the Mishnah are preserved either as narrative settings for the statement of the law, or, occasionally, as precedents.

Historical events are classified and turned into entries on lists. But incidents in any case come few and far between. True, events do make an impact. But it always is for the Mishnah's own purpose and within its own taxonomic system and rule-seeking mode of thought. To be sure, the framers of the Mishnah may also have had a theory of the Messiah and of the meaning of Israel's history and destiny. But they kept it hidden, and their document manages to provide an immense account of Israel's life without explicitly telling us about such matters.

The Mishnah sets forth the decline of generations, in which the destruction of the Temple and the death of great sages mark the movement of time and impart to an age the general rules that govern life therein. Here is how the Messiah-theme is treated by the Mishnah:

MISHNAH-TRACTATE SOTAH 9:15

A. When R. Meir died, makers of parables came to an end.

B. When Ben Azzai died, diligent students came to an end.

C. When Ben Zoma died, exegetes came to an end.

D. When R. Joshua died, goodness went away from the world.

E. When Rabban Simeon b. Gamaliel died, the locust came, and troubles multiplied.

F. When Eleazar b. Azariah died, wealth went away from the sages.

G. When R. Aqiba died, the glory of the Torah came to an end.

H. When R. Hanina b. Dosa died, wonder-workers came to an end.

I. When R. Yosé Qatnuta died, pietists went away.

J. (And why was he called *Qatnuta?* Because he was the least of the pietists.)

K. When Rabban Yohanan b. Zakkai died, the splendor of wisdom came to an end.

L. When Rabban Gamaliel the Elder died, the glory of the Torah came to an end, and cleanness and separateness perished.

M. When R. Ishmael b. Phabi died, the splendor of the priesthood came to an end.

N. When Rabbi died, modesty and fear of sin came to an end.

O. R. Pinhas b. Yair says, "When the Temple was destroyed, associates became ashamed and so did free men, and they covered their heads.

P. "And wonder-workers became feeble. And violent men and big takers grew strong.

Q. "And none expounds and none seeks [learning] and none asks.

R.　"Upon whom shall we depend? Upon our Father in heaven."

S.　R. Eliezer the Great says, "From the day on which the Temple was destroyed, sages began to be like scribes, and scribes like ministers, and ministers like ordinary folk.

T.　"And the ordinary folk have become feeble.

U.　"And none seeks.

V.　"Upon whom shall we depend? Upon our Father in heaven."

W.　With the footprints of the Messiah: presumption increases, and dearth increases.

X.　The Vine gives its fruit and wine at great cost.

Y.　And the government turns to heresy.

Z.　And there is no reproof.

AA.　The gathering place will be for prostitution.

BB.　And Galilee will be laid waste.

CC.　And the Gablan will be made desolate.

DD.　And the men of the frontier will go about from town to town, and none will take pity on them.

EE.　And the wisdom of scribes will putrefy.

FF.　And those who fear sin will be rejected.

GG.　And the truth will be locked away.

HH.　Children will shame elders, and elders will stand up before children.

II.　"For the son dishonors the father and the daughter rises up against her mother, the daughter-in-law against her mother-in-law; a man's enemies are the men of his own house" (Mic. 7:6).

JJ.　The face of the generation in the face of a dog.

KK.　A son is not ashamed before his father.

LL.　Upon whom shall we depend? Upon our Father in heaven.

MM.　R. Pinhas b. Yair says, "Heedfulness leads to cleanliness, cleanliness leads to cleanness, cleanness leads to abstinence, abstinence leads to holiness, holiness leads to modesty, modesty leads to the fear of sin, the fear of sin leads to piety, piety leads to the Holy Spirit, the Holy Spirit leads to the resurrection of the dead, and the resurrection of the dead comes through Elijah, blessed be his memory, Amen."

The Messiah in the Mishnah does not stand at the forefront of the framers' consciousness. The issues encapsulated in the myth and person of the Messiah are scarcely addressed. The framers of the Mishnah do not resort to speculation about the Messiah as a historical-supernatural figure. So far as that kind of speculation provides the vehicle for reflection on salvific issues, or in mythic terms, narratives on the meaning of history and the destiny of Israel, we cannot say that the Mishnah's philosophers take up those encompassing categories of being: Where are we heading? What can we do about it? That does not mean questions found urgent in the aftermath of the destruction of the Temple and the disaster of Bar Kokhba failed to attract the attention of the Mishnah's sages. But they treated history in a different way, offering their own answers to its questions. To these we now turn.

When it comes to history and the end of time, the Mishnah absorbs into its encompassing system all events, small and large. With them the sages accomplish what they accomplish in everything else: a vast labor of taxonomy, an immense construction of the order and rules governing the classification of everything on earth and in heaven. The disruptive character of history — onetime events of ineluctable significance — scarcely impresses the philosophers. They find no difficulty in showing that what appears unique and beyond classification has in fact happened before and so falls within the range of trustworthy rules and known procedures. Once history's components, onetime events, lose their distinctiveness, then history as a didactic intellectual construct, as a source of lessons and rules, also loses all pertinence.

So lessons and rules come from sorting things out and classifying them from the procedures and modes of thought of the philosopher seeking regularity. To this labor of taxonomy, the historian's way of selecting data and arranging them into patterns of meaning to teach lessons proves inconsequential. Onetime events are not important. The world is composed of nature and supernature. The laws that count are those to be discovered in heaven and, in heaven's creation and counterpart, on earth. Keep those laws and things will work out. Break them, and the result is predictable: calamity of whatever sort will supervene in accordance with the rules. But just because it is predictable, a catastrophic happening testifies to what has always been and must always be, in accordance with reliable rules and within categories already discovered and well explained. That is why the lawyer-philosophers of the mid-second century produced the Mishnah — to explain how things are. Within the framework of well-classified rules, there could be Messiahs, but no single Messiah.

II. THE MESSIAH-THEME IN ABOT

If the end of time and the coming of the Messiah do not serve to explain, for the Mishnah's system, why people should do what the Mishnah says, then what alternative teleology does the Mishnah's first apologetic, Abot, provide? Only when we appreciate the clear answers given in that document, brought to closure at ca. 250, shall we grasp how remarkable is the shift, which took place in later documents of the rabbinic canon, to a messianic framing of the issues of the Torah's ultimate purpose and value. Let us see how the framers of Abot, in the aftermath of the creation of the Mishnah, explain the purpose and goal of the Mishnah: an ahistorical, non-messianic teleology.

The first document generated by the Mishnah's heirs took up the work of completing the Mishnah's system by answering questions of purpose and meaning. Whatever teleology the Mishnah as such would ever acquire would derive from Abot, which presents statements to express the ethos and ethic of the Mishnah, and so provides a kind of theory. Abot agreed with the other sixty-two tractates: history proved no more important here than it had been before. With scarcely a word about history and no account of events at all, Abot manages to provide an ample account of how the Torah — written and oral, thus in later eyes, Scripture and Mishnah — came down to its own day. Accordingly, the passage of time as such plays no role in the explanation of the origins of the document, nor is the Mishnah presented as eschatological.

Occurrences of great weight ("history") are never invoked. How then does the tractate tell the story of Torah, narrate the history of God's revelation to Israel, encompassing both Scripture and Mishnah? The answer is that Abot's framers manage to do their work of explanation without telling a story or invoking history at all. They pursue a different way of answering the same question, by exploiting a non-historical mode of thought and method of legitimation. And that is the main point: teleology serves the purpose of legitimation, and hence is accomplished in ways other than explaining how things originated or assuming that historical fact explains anything.

In the Mishnah, time is differentiated entirely in other than national-historical categories. For, as in Abot, "this world" is when one is alive, "the world to come" is when a person dies. True, we find also "this world" and "the time of the Messiah." But detailed differentiation among the ages of "this world" or "this age" hardly generates problems in Mishnaic thought. Indeed, no such differentiation appears. Accordingly, the developments briefly outlined here constitute a significant shift in the course of intellectual events, to which the sources at hand — the Mishnah and Talmud of the Land of Israel — amply testify. In ca. A. D. 200 events posed a problem of classification and generalization. In ca. A. D. 400, events were singular and demanded interpretation because, in all their particularity, they bore messages just as, in prophetic thought, they had. In the reconsideration of the singularity of events and the systematic effort at interpreting them and the lessons to be drawn from them, the sages of the Talmud of the Land of Israel regained for their theological thought the powerful resources of history, the single most powerful arena for, and principal medium of, Judaic theology then as now.

III. THE ADVENT OF THE MESSIAH: THE TALMUD OF THE LAND OF ISRAEL

By this point in our examination of the system of Rabbinic Judaism — its account not of how things are but of how they work — we cannot find surprising the simple fact that the Messiah-theme, trivial in the Mishnah, moves to the forefront in the Yerushalmi. That correlates with the same document's keen interest in history and its patterns. If the Mishnah provided a teleology without eschatology, the framers of the Yerushalmi and related Midrash-compilations could not conceive of any but an utterly eschatological goal for themselves. Historical events entered into the construction of a teleology for the Yerushalmi's system of Judaism as a whole. What the law demanded reflected the consequences of wrongful action on the part of Israel. So, again, Israel's own deeds defined the events of history. Rome's role, like Assyria's and Babylonia's, depended upon Israel's provoking divine wrath as it was executed by the great empires. This mode of thought comes to simple expression in what follows.

YERUSHALMI ERUBIN 3:9
[IV B]   R. Ba, R. Hiyya in the name of R. Yohanan: "'Do not gaze at me because I am swarthy, because the sun has scorched me. My mother's sons were angry with me, they made me keeper of the vineyards; but, my own vineyard, I have not kept!' [Song 1:6]. What made me guard the vineyards? It is because of not keeping my own vineyard.

[C]   What made me keep two festival days in Syria? It is because I did not keep the proper festival day in the Holy Land.

[D]   "I imagined that I would receive a reward for the two days, but I received a reward only for one of them.

[E]   "Who made it necessary that I should have to separate two pieces of dough-offering from grain grown in Syria? It is because I did not separate a single piece of dough-offering in the Land of Israel."

Israel had to learn the lesson of its history to also take command of its own destiny.

But this notion of determining one's own destiny should not be misunderstood. The framers of the Talmud of the Land of Israel were not telling the Jews to please God by doing commandments in order that they should thereby gain control of their own destiny. To the contrary, the paradox of the Yerushalmi's system lies in the fact that Israel can free itself of control by other nations only by humbly agreeing to accept God's rule. The nations — Rome, in the present instance — rest on one side of the balance, while God rests on the other. Israel must then choose between them. There is no such thing for Israel as freedom from both God and the nations, total autonomy and independence. There is only a choice of masters, a ruler on earth or a ruler in heaven.

With propositions such as these, the framers of the Mishnah will certainly have concurred. And why not? For the fundamental affirmations of the Mishnah about the centrality of Israel's perfection in stasis — sanctification — readily prove congruent to the attitudes at hand. Once the Messiah's coming had become dependent upon Israel's condition and not upon Israel's actions in historical time, then the Mishnah's system will have imposed its fundamental and definitive character upon the Messiah-myth. An eschatological teleology framed through that myth then would prove wholly appropriate to the method of the larger system of the Mishnah. That is for a simple, striking reason. The Messiah-theme is made to repeat, in its terms, the doctrine of virtuous attitudes and emotions that prevail throughout; the condition of the coming of the Messiah is Israel's humility, its submission to the tides and currents of history. What, after all, makes a Messiah a false Messiah? In this Talmud, it is not his claim to save Israel, but his claim to save Israel without the help of God. The meaning of the true Messiah is Israel's total submission, through the Messiah's gentle rule, to God's yoke and service. So God is not to be manipulated through Israel's humoring of heaven in rite and cult.

The notion of keeping the commandments so as to please heaven and get God to do what Israel wants is totally incongruent to the text at hand. Keeping the commandments as a mark of submission, loyalty, humility before God is the rabbinic system of salvation. So Israel does not "save itself." Israel never controls its own destiny, either on earth or in heaven. The only choice is whether to cast one's fate into the hands of cruel, deceitful men, or to trust in the living God of mercy and love. The stress that Israel's arrogance alienates God, Israel's humility and submission win God's favor, cannot surprise us; this is the very point of the doctrine of emotions that defines Rabbinic Judaism's ethics. Now the same view is expressed in a still more critical area. We shall now see how this position is spelled out in the setting of discourse about the Messiah in the Talmud of the Land of Israel.

The failed Messiah of the second century, Bar Kokhba, above all exemplifies arrogance against God. He lost the war because of that arrogance. His emotions, attitudes, sentiments, and feelings form the model of how the virtuous Israelite is not to conceive of matters. In particular, he ignored the authority of sages:

YERUSHALMI TAANIT 4:5

[X J] Said R. Yohanan, "Upon orders of Caesar Hadrian, they killed eight hundred thousand in Betar."

[K] Said R. Yohanan, "There were eighty thousand pairs of trumpeters surrounding Betar. Each one was in charge of a number of troops. Ben Kozeba was there and he had two hundred thousand troops who, as a sign of loyalty, had cut off their little fingers.

[L] "Sages sent word to him, 'How long are you going to turn Israel into a maimed people.

[M] "He said to them, 'How otherwise is it possible to test them?'

[N] "They replied to him, 'Whoever cannot uproot a cedar of Lebanon while riding on his horse will not be inscribed on your military rolls.'

[O] "So there were two hundred thousand who qualified in one way, and another two hundred thousand who qualified in another way."

[P]   When he would go forth to battle, he would say, "Lord of the world! Do not help and do not hinder us! 'Hast thou not rejected us, O God? Thou dost not go forth, O God, with our armies'"[Ps. 60:10].

[Q]   Three-and-a-half years did Hadrian besiege Betar.

[R]   R. Eleazar of Modiin would sit on sackcloth and ashes and pray every day, saying "Lord of the ages! Do not judge in accord with strict judgment this day! Do not judge in accord with strict judgment this day!"

[S]   Hadrian wanted to go to him. A Samaritan said to him, "Do not go to him until I see what he is doing, and so hand over the city [of Betar] to you. [Make peace ... for you.]"

[T]   [The Samaritan] got into the city through a drainpipe. He went and found R. Eleazar of Modiin standing and praying. He pretended to whisper something in his ear.

[U]   The townspeople saw [the Samaritan] do this and brought him to Ben Kozeba. They told him, "We saw this man having dealings with your friend."

[V]   [Bar Kokhba] said to him, "What did you say to him, and what did he say to you?"

[W]   He said to [the Samaritan], "If I tell you, then the king will kill me, and if I do not tell you, then you will kill me. It is better that the king kill me, and not you.

[X]   "[Eleazar] said to me, 'I should hand over my city.' ['I shall make peace ....']"

[Y]   He turned to R. Eleazar of Modiin. He said to him, "What did this Samaritan say to you?"

[Z]   He replied, "Nothing."

[AA] He said to him, "What did you say to him?"

[BB] He said to him, "Nothing."

[CC] [Ben Kozeba] gave [Eleazar] one good kick and killed him.

[DD] Forthwith an echo came forth and proclaimed the following verse:

[EE] "Woe to my worthless shepherd, who deserts the flock! May the sword smite his arm and his right eye! Let his arm be wholly withered, his right eye utterly blinded! [Zech. 11:17].

[FF] "You have murdered R. Eleazar of Modiin, the right arm of all Israel, and their right eye. Therefore may the right arm of that man wither, may his right eye be utterly blinded!"

[GG] Forthwith Betar was taken, and Ben Kozeba was killed.

That kick — an act of temper, a demonstration of untamed emotions — tells the whole story. We notice two complementary themes. First, Bar Kokhba treats heaven with arrogance, asking God merely to keep out of the way. Second, he treats an especially revered sage with a parallel arrogance. The sage had the power to preserve Israel. Bar Kokhba destroyed Israel's one protection. The result was inevitable.

The Messiah, the centerpiece of salvation history and hero of the tale, emerged as a critical figure. The historical theory of this Yerushalmi passage is stated very simply. In their view Israel had to choose between wars, either the war fought by Bar Kokhba or the "war for Torah." "Why had they been punished? It was because of the weight of the war, for they had not wanted to engage in the struggles over the meaning of the Torah" (Yerushalmi Ta. 3:9 XVI I). Those struggles, which were ritual arguments about ritual matters, promised the only victory worth winning. Then Israel's history would be written in terms of wars over the meaning of the Torah and the decision of the law.

The Talmud of Babylonia, at the end, carried forward the innovations we have seen in the Talmud of the Land of Israel. In the view expressed here, the principal result of Israel's loyal adherence to the Torah and its religious duties will be Israel's humble acceptance of God's rule. The humility, under all conditions, makes God love Israel.

Babli Hullin 89a

"It was not because you were greater than any people that the Lord set his love upon you and chose you" [Deut. 7:7]. The Holy One, blessed be he, said to Israel, "I love you because even when I bestow greatness upon you, you humble yourselves before me. I bestowed greatness upon Abraham, yet he said to me, 'I am but dust and ashes' [Gen. 18:27]; upon Moses and Aaron, yet they said, 'But I am a worm and no man' [Ps. 22:7]. But with the heathens it is not so. I bestowed greatness upon Nimrod, and he said, 'Come, let us build us a city' [Gen. 11:4]; upon Pharaoh, and he said, 'Who are they among all the gods of the countries?' [2 Kings 18:35]; upon Nebuchadnezzar, and he said, 'I will ascend above the heights of the clouds' [Isa. 14:14]; upon Hiram, king of Tyre, and he said, 'I sit in the seat of God, in the heart of the seas' [Ezek. 28:2]."

So the system emerges complete, each of its parts stating precisely the same message as is revealed in the whole. The issue of the Messiah and the meaning of Israel's history framed through the Messiah-myth convey in their terms precisely the same position that we find everywhere else in all other symbolic components of the rabbinic system and canon. The heart of the matter then is Israel's subservience to God's will, as expressed in the Torah and embodied in the teachings and lives of the great sages. When Israel fully accepts God's rule, then the Messiah will come. Until Israel subjects itself to God's rule, the Jews will be subjugated to pagan domination. Since the condition of Israel governs, Israel itself holds the key to its own redemption. But this it can achieve only by throwing away the key!

What we have is a very concrete way of formulating the relationship that yields *zekhut:* negotiation, conciliation, not dominance, not assertiveness. The paradox must be crystal clear: Israel acts to redeem itself through the opposite of self-determination, namely, by subjugating itself to God. Israel's power lies in its negation of power. Its destiny lies in giving up all pretense at deciding its own destiny. So weakness is the ultimate strength, forbearance the final act of self-assertion, passive resignation the sure step toward liberation. (The parallel is the crucified Christ.) Israel's freedom is engraved on the tablets of the commandments of God: to be free is freely to obey. That is not the meaning associated with these words in the minds of others who, like the sages of the rabbinical canon, declared their view of what Israel must do to secure the coming of the Messiah.

The passage, praising Israel for its humility, completes the circle begun with the description of Bar Kokhba as arrogant and boastful. Gentile kings are boastful; Israelite kings are humble. So, in all, the Messiah-myth deals with a very concrete and limited consideration of the national life and character. The theory of Israel's history and destiny as it was expressed within that myth interprets matters in terms of a single criterion. What others within the Israelite world had done or in the future would do with the conviction that, at the end of time, God would send a (or the) Messiah to "save" Israel, it was a single idea for the sages of the Mishnah and the Talmuds and collections of scriptural exegesis. And that conception stands at the center of their system; it shapes and is shaped by their system. In context, the Messiah expresses the system's meaning and so makes it work.

The appearance of a messianic eschatology fully consonant with the larger characteristic of the rabbinic system — with its stress on the viewpoints and prooftexts of Scripture, its interest in what was happening to Israel, its focus upon the national-historical dimension of the life of the group — indicates that the encompassing rabbinic system stands essentially autonomous of the prior Mishnaic system. True, what had gone before was absorbed and fully assimilated, but the rabbinic system first appearing in the Talmud of the Land of Israel is different in the aggregate from the Mishnaic system. It represents more, however, than a negative response to its predecessor. The rabbinic system of the two Talmuds took over the fundamental convictions of the Mishnaic worldview about the importance of Israel's constructing for itself a life beyond time.

The rabbinic system then transformed the Messiah-myth in its totality into an essentially ahistorical force. If people wanted to reach the end of time, they had to rise above time, that is, history, and stand off at the side of great movements of political and military character. That is the message of the Messiah-myth as it reaches full exposure in the rabbinic system of the two Talmuds. At its foundation it is precisely the message of teleology without eschatology expressed by the Mishnah and its associated documents. Accordingly, we cannot claim that the rabbinic or talmudic system in this regard constitutes a reaction against the Mishnaic one. We must conclude, quite to the contrary, that in the Talmuds and their associated documents we see the restatement in classical-mythic form of the ontological convictions that had informed the minds of the second-century philosophers. The new medium contained the old and enduring message: Israel must turn away from time and change, submit to whatever happens, so as to win for itself the only government worth having, that is, God's rule, accomplished through God's anointed agent, the Messiah.

In the Talmud's theory of salvation the framers provided Israel with an account of how to overcome the unsatisfactory circumstances of an unredeemed present, so as to accomplish the movement from here to the much-desired future. When the Talmud's authorities present statements on the promise of the law for those who keep it, therefore, they provide glimpses of the goal of the system as a whole. These invoked the primacy of the rabbi and the legitimating power of the Torah, and in those two components of the system we find the principles of the Messianic doctrine. And these bring us back to the argument with Christ triumphant, as the Christians perceived him.

IV. MESSIAH IN CONTEXT, THE CHRISTIAN CHALLENGE

Once more we ask about the relationship of text to context, finding in the circumstance a way of explaining the substance of the functioning system before us. The context in which the Talmud of the Land of Israel and related Midrash-compilations restated the received Messiah-theme, defining the Messiah as a humble sage finds its definition in the triumph of Christianity. The government's adoption of Christianity as the state religion was taken to validate the Christian claim that Jesus was, and is, Christ. Indeed, every page of Eusebius' writing bears the message that the conversion of Constantine proves the Christhood of Jesus: his messianic standing. History — the affairs of nations and monarchs — yields laws of society, proves God's will, and matters now speak for themselves. For Judaism the dramatic shift in the fortunes of the competing biblical faith raised a simple and unpleasant possibility: perhaps Israel had been wrong after all. Since the Jews as a whole, and sages among them, anticipated the coming of the Messiah promised by the prophets, the issue could be fairly joined. If history proves propositions, as the prophets and apocalyptic visionaries had maintained, then how could Jews deny the Christians' claim that the conversion of the emperor, then of the Empire, demonstrated the true state of affairs in heaven as much as on earth?

John Chrysostom, who stands for Christianity on the messianic issue, typifies the Christian theologians' concern that converts not proceed to the synagogue or retain connections with it. For the burden of his case was that since Christ had now been proved Messiah, Christians no longer could associate themselves with the synagogue. Judaism had lost, Christianity had won, and people had to choose the one and give up the other. At stake for Chrysostom, whose sermons on Judaism, preached in 386-87, provide for our purpose the statement of Christianity on the Messianic issue, was Christians' participation in synagogue rites and Judaic practices. He invoked the Jews' failure in the fiasco of the proposed rebuilding of the Temple in Jerusalem only a quarter of a century earlier. He drew upon the failure of that project to demonstrate that Judaic rites no longer held any power. He further cited that incident to prove that Israel's salvation lay wholly in the past, in the time of the return to Zion, and never in the future. So the happenings of the day demonstrated proofs of the faith. The struggle between sages and theologians concerned the meaning of important contemporary happenings, and the same happenings, read in light of the same Scripture, provoked discussion of the same issues: a confrontation.

The messianic crisis confronting the Christian theologians hardly matches that facing the Judaic sages. The one dealt with problems of triumph, the other, despair; the one had to interpret a new day, the other to explain disaster. Scripture explicitly promised that Israel would receive salvation from God's anointed Messiah at the end of time. The teleology of Israelite faith, in the biblical account, focused upon eschatology, and, within eschatology, on the salvific, therefore the messianic, dimension. On the other hand, the Mishnah had for its part taken up a view of its own on the issue of teleology, presenting an ahistorical and essentially non-messianic teleology. Sages' response to the messianic crisis had to mediate two distinct and contradictory positions. Sages explained what the messianic hope now entailed, and how to identify the Messiah, who would be a sage. They further included the messianic issue in their larger historical theory. So we cannot address the question at hand as if the Christians defined the agendum. True, to Israel all they had to say was, "Why not?" But sages responded with a far-reaching doctrine of their own, deeming the question, in its Christian formulation, trivial.

But the issue confronting both Judaic sages and Christian theologians was one and the same: precisely what difference the Messiah makes. To state matters as they would be worked out by both parties, in the light of the events of the day: what do I have to do because the Messiah has come (Christian) or because I want the Messiah to come (Judaic)? That question encompasses two sides of a single issue. On the issue of the Messiahship of Jesus all other matters depended. It follows that one party believed precisely the opposite of the other on an issue shared in identical definition by both. For Christians, the sole issue — belief or unbelief — carried a clear implication for the audience subject to address. When debate would go forward, it would center upon the wavering of Christians and the unbelief of Jews. Our exemplary figure, Chrysostom, framed matters in those terms, drawing upon the events of his own day for ample instantiation of the matter. The Christian formulation thus focused all argument on the vindication of Jesus as Christ. When Christians found attractive aspects of Judaic rite and belief, the Christian theologians invoked the fundamental issue: is Jesus Christ? If so, then Judaism falls. If not, then Christianity fails. No question, therefore, drew the two sets of intellectuals into more direct conflict; none bore so immediate and fundamental consequences. Christians did not have to keep the Torah — that was a principal message of Chrysostom in context.

The Christian challenge is what stimulated sages' thought to focus upon the Messiah-theme. The Mishnaic system had come to full expression without an elaborated doctrine of the Messiah, or even an eschatological theory of the purpose and goal of matters. The Mishnah had put forth (in tractate Abot) a teleology without an eschatological dimension at all. By the closing of the Talmud of the Land of Israel, by contrast, the purpose and end of everything centered upon the coming of the Messiah, in sages' terms and definition, to be sure. That is surprising in light of the character of the Mishnah's system, to which the Talmud of the Land of Israel attached itself as a commentary.

In order to understand sages' development of the Messiah-theme in the Talmud of the Land of Israel, therefore, we have to backtrack and consider how the theme had made its appearance in the Mishnah. Only in comparison to its earlier expression and use therefore does the Talmud's formulation of the matter enter proper context for interpretation Critical issues of teleology had been worked out through messianic eschatology in other, earlier Judaic systems. Later ones as well would invoke the Messiah-theme. These systems, including the Christian one , resorted to the myth of the Messiah as savior and redeemer of Israel, a supernatural figure engaged in political-historical tasks as king of the Jews, even a God-man facing the crucial historical questions of Israel's life and then resolving them — Christ as king of the world, of the ages, even of death itself.

v. IDENTIFYING THE MESSIAH, HASTENING HIS ADVENT

In the Talmud of the Land of Israel, ca. A.D. 400, we find a fully exposed doctrine not only of a Messiah (e.g., a kind of priest or general), but of *the* Messiah, the one man who will save Israel: who he is, how we will know him, what we must do to bring him. It follows that the Talmud of the Land of Israel presents clear evidence that the Messiah-myth had found its place within that larger Torah-myth that characterized Judaism in its later formative literature. A clear effort to identify the person of the Messiah and to confront the claim that a specific, named individual had been, or would be, the Messiah — these come to the fore. This means that the issue had reached the center of lively discourse at least in some rabbinic circles. the disposition of the issue proves distinctive to sages: the Messiah will be a sage, the Messiah will come when Israel has attained that condition of sanctification, marked also by profound humility and complete acceptance of God's will, that signify sanctification.

These two conditions say the same thing twice: sages' Judaism will identify the Messiah and teach how to bring him nearer. In these allegations we find no point of intersection with issues important to Chrysostom, even though the Talmud of the Land of Israel reached closure at the same time as Chrysostom's preaching. For Chrysostom dealt with the Messiah-theme in terms pertinent to his larger system, and sages did the same. But the issue was fairly joined. In Chrysostom's terms, it was: Jesus is Christ, proved by the events of the recent past. In sages' terms it was: the Messiah will be a sage, coming when Israel fully accepts, in all humility, God's sole rule. The first stage in the position of each hardly matches that in the outline of the other. But the second does: Jesus is Christ, therefore Israel will have no other Messiah. The Messiah will come, in the form of a sage, and therefore no one who now claims to be the Messiah is in fact the savior.

Issues are joined in a confrontation of ideas. There is a clear fit between one side's framing of the Messiah-theme and the other party's framing of the same theme. And we cannot forget that larger context in which the theme worked itself out: the Messiah joined to the doctrine of history and of Israel, fore and aft, forms a large and integrated picture. If Jesus is Christ, then history has come to its fulfillment and Israel is no longer God's people. The sages' counterpart system: the Messiah has not yet come, history as the sequence of empires has in store yet one more age, the age of Israel, and Israel remains the family, the children of Abraham, Isaac, and Jacob. So Christianity, so Judaism: both confronted precisely the same issues defined in exactly the same way.

In the Talmud of the Land of Israel two historical contexts framed discussion of the Messiah, the destruction of the Temple, as with Chrysostom's framing of the issue, and the messianic claim of Bar Kokhba. Rome played a role in both, and the authors of the materials gathered in the Talmud made a place for Rome in the history of Israel. This they did in conformity to their larger theory of who is Israel, specifically by assigning to Rome a place in the family. As to the destruction of the Temple, we find a statement that the Messiah was born on the day that the Temple was destroyed. The Talmud's doctrine of the Messiah therefore finds its place in its encompassing doctrine of history. What is fresh in the Talmud is the perception of Rome as an autonomous actor, as an entity with a point of origin (just as Israel has a point of origin) and a tradition of wisdom (just as Israel has such a tradition). So as Rome is Esau, so Esau is part of the family — a point to which we shall return — and therefore plays a role in history. And — yet another point of considerable importance — since Rome does play a role in history, Rome also finds a position in the eschatological drama. This sense of poised opposites, Israel and Rome, comes to expression in two ways. First, Israel's own history calls into being its counterpart, the anti-history of Rome. Without Israel, there would be no Rome — a wonderful consolation to the defeated nation. For if Israel's sin created Rome's power, then Israel's repentance would bring Rome's downfall. Here is the way in which the Talmud presents the match:

The concept of two histories, balanced opposite one another, comes to particular expression, within the Talmud of the Land of Israel, in the balance of Israelite sage and Roman emperor. Just as Israel and Rome, God and no-gods, compete (with a foreordained conclusion), so do sage and emperor. In this age, it appears that the emperor has the power. God's Temple, by contrast to the great Churches of the age, lies in ruins. But just as sages can overcome the emperor through their inherent supernatural power, so too will Israel and Israel's God in the coming age control the course of events. In the doctrine at hand, we see the true balance: sage as against emperor. In the age of the Christian emperors, the polemic acquires power.

The sage, in his small claims court, weighs in the balance against the emperor in Constantinople — a rather considerable claim. So two stunning innovations appear: first, the notion of emperor and sage in mortal struggle; second, the idea of an age of idolatry and an age beyond idolatry. The world had to move into a new orbit indeed for Rome to enter into the historical context formerly defined wholly by what happened to Israel. How does all this relate to the Messianic crisis at hand? The doctrine of sages, directly pertinent to the issue of the coming of the Messiah, holds that Israel can free itself of control by other nations only by humbly agreeing to accept God's rule. The nations — Rome, in the present instance — rest on one side of the balance, while God rests on the other. Israel must then choose between them. There is no such thing for Israel as freedom from both God and the nations, total autonomy and independence. There is only a choice of masters, a ruler on earth or a ruler in heaven.

Once the figure of the Messiah has come on stage, there arises discussion on who, among the living, the Messiah might be. The identification of the Messiah begins with the person of David himself: "If the Messiah-King comes from among the living, his name will be David. If he comes from among the dead, it will be King David himself" (Yerushalmi Ber. 2:3 V P). A variety of evidence announced the advent of the Messiah as a figure in the larger system of formative Judaism. The rabbinization of David constitutes one kind of evidence. Serious discussion, within the framework of the accepted documents of Mishnaic exegesis and the law, concerning the identification and claim of diverse figures asserted to be Messiahs, presents still more telling proof.

YERUSHALMI BERAKHOT 2:4
(TRANSLATED BY T. ZAHAVY)

[A] Once a Jew was plowing and his ox snorted once before him. An Arab who was passing and heard the sound said to him, "Jew, loosen your ox and loosen the plow and stop plowing. For today your Temple was destroyed."

[B] The ox snorted again. He [the Arab] said to him, "Jew, bind your ox and bind your plow, for today the Messiah-King was born."

[C] He said to him, "What is his name?"

[D] "Menahem."

[E] He said to him, "And what is his father's name?"

[F] The Arab said to him, "Hezekiah."

[G] He said to him, "Where is he from?"

[H] He said to him, "From the royal capital of Bethlehem in Judea."

[I]   The Jew went and sold his ox and sold his plow. And he became a peddler of infant's felt-cloths [diapers]. And he went from place to place until he came to that very city. All of the women bought from him. But Menahem's mother did not buy from him.

[J]   He heard the women saying, "Menahem's mother, Menahem's mother, come buy for your child."

[K]   She said, "I want to bring him up to hate Israel. For on the day he was born, the Temple was destroyed."

[L]   They said to her, "We are sure that on this day it was destroyed, and on this day of the year it will be rebuilt."

[M]   She said to the peddler, "I have no money."

[N]   He said to her, "It is of no matter to me. Come and buy for him and pay me when I return."

[O]   A while later he returned to that city. He said to her, "How is the infant doing?"

[P]   She said to him, "Since the time you saw him a spirit came and carried him away from me."

[Q]   Said R. Bun, "Why do we learn this from [a story about] an Arab? Do we not have explicit scriptural evidence for it? 'Lebanon with its majestic trees will fall' [Isa. 10:34]. And what follows this? 'There shall come forth a shoot from the stump of Jesse' [Isa. 11:1]. [Right after an allusion to the destruction of the Temple the prophet speaks of the messianic age.]"

This is a set-piece story, adduced to prove that the Messiah was born on the day the Temple was destroyed. The Messiah was born when the Temple was destroyed; hence, God prepared for Israel a better fate than had appeared.

A more concrete matter — the identification of the Messiah with a known historical personality — was associated with the name of Aqiba. He is said to have claimed that Bar Kokhba, leader of the second-century revolt, was the Messiah. The important aspect of the story, however, is the rejection of Aqiba's view. The discredited Messiah figure (if Bar Kokhba actually was such in his own day) finds no apologists in the later rabbinical canon. What is striking in what follows, moreover, is that we really have two stories. At G Aqiba is said to have believed that Bar Kokhba was a disappointment. At H-I, he is said to have identified Bar Kokhba with the King-Messiah. Both cannot be true, so what we have is simply two separate opinions of Aqiba's judgment of Bar Kokhba/Bar Kozebah.

Yerushalmi Taanit 4:5

[X G]   R. Simeon b. Yohai taught, "Aqiba, my master, would interpret the following verse: 'A star (*kokhab*) shall come forth out of

Jacob' [Num. 24:17] "A disappointment (*Kozeba*) shall come forth out of Jacob.'"

[H]   R. Aqiba, when he saw Bar Kozeba, said, "This is the King Messiah."

[I]   R. Yohanan ben Toreta said to him, "Aqiba! Grass will grow on your cheeks before the Messiah will come!"

The important point is not only that Aqiba had been proved wrong. It is that the very verse of Scripture adduced in behalf of his viewpoint could be treated more generally and made to refer to righteous people in general, not to the Messiah in particular. And that leads us to the issue of the age, as sages' had to face it: what makes a Messiah a false Messiah? The answer, we recall, is arrogance.

Now we should not conclude that the Talmud at hand has simply moved beyond the Mishnah's orbit. The opposite is the case. What the framers of the document have done is to assemble materials in which the eschatological, therefore Messianic, teleology is absorbed within the ahistorical, therefore sagacious one. The Messiah turned into a sage is no longer the Messiah embodied in the figure of the arrogant Bar Kokhba (in the Talmud's representation of the figure). The reversion to the prophetic notion of learning history's lessons carried in its wake a re-engagement with the Messiah-myth. But the re-engagement does not represent a change in the unfolding system. Why not? Because the climax comes in an explicit statement that the conduct required by the Torah will bring the coming Messiah. That explanation of the holy way of life focuses upon the end of time and the advent of the Messiah — both of which therefore depend upon the sanctification of Israel. So sanctification takes priority, salvation depends on it. The framers of the Mishnah had found it possible to construct a complete and encompassing teleology for their system with scarcely a single word about the Messiah's coming at that time when the system would be perfectly achieved.

The Yerushalmi, heir to the Mishnah, accomplished the re-messianization of the system of Rabbinic Judaism. The reversion to the prophetic notion of learning the lessons of history carried in its wake re-engagement with the Messiah-myth. The climax of the matter comes in an explicit statement that the practice of conduct required by the Torah will bring about the coming of the Messiah. That explanation of the purpose of the holy way of life, focused now upon the end of time and the advent of the Messiah, must strike us as surprising. For the framers of the Mishnah had found it possible to construct a complete and encompassing teleology for their system with scarcely a single word about the Messiah's coming when the system would be perfectly achieved. So with their interest in explaining events and accounting for history, third- and-fourth-century sages represented in the units of discourse at hand invoked what their predecessors had at best found of peripheral consequence to their system. The following contains the most striking expression of the viewpoint at hand.

YERUSHALMI TAANIT 1:1

X. J. "The oracle concerning Dumah. One is calling to me from Seir, 'Watchman, what of the night? Watchman, what of the night?' (Is. 21:11)."

K. The Israelites said to Isaiah, "O our Rabbi, Isaiah, what will come for us out of this night?"

L. He said to them, "Wait for me, until I can present the question."

M. Once he had asked the question, he came back to them.

N. They said to him, "Watchman, what of the night? What did the Guardian of the ages tell you?"

O. He said to them, "The watchman says" 'Morning comes; and also the night. If you will inquire, inquire; come back again' (Is. 21:12)."

P. They said to him, "Also the night?"

Q. He said to them, "It is not what you are thinking. But there will be morning for the righteous, and night for the wicked, morning for Israel, and night for idolaters."

R. They said to him, "When?"

S. He said to them, "Whenever you want, He too wants [it to be] — if you want it, he wants it."

T. They said to him, "What is standing in the way?"

U. He said to them, "Repentance: 'Come back again' (Is. 21:12)."

V. R. Aha in the name of R. Tanhum b. R. Hiyya, "If Israel repents for one day, forthwith the son of David will come.

W. "What is the Scriptural basis? 'O that today you would hearken to his voice!' (Ps. 95:7)."

X. Said R. Levi, "If Israel would keep a single Sabbath in the proper way, forthwith the son of David will come.

Y. "What is the Scriptural basis for this view? 'Moses said, Eat it today, for today is a Sabbath to the Lord; today you will not find it in the field' (Ex. 16:25).

Z. "And it says, 'For thus said the Lord God, the Holy One of Israel, 'In returning and rest you shall be saved; in quietness and in trust shall be your strength.' And you would not' (Is. 30:15)."

The discussion of the power of repentance would hardly have surprised a Mishnah-sage. What is new is at V-Z, the explicit linkage of keeping the law with achieving the end of time and the coming of the Messiah. That motif stands separate from the notions of righteousness and repentance, which surely do not require it. So the condition of "all Israel," a social category in historical time, comes under consideration, and not only the status of individual Israelites in life and in death. The latter had formed the arena for Abot's account of the Mishnah's meaning.

Now history as an operative category, drawing in its wake Israel as a social entity, comes once more on the scene. But, except for the Mishnah's sages, it had never left the stage.

We must not lose sight of the importance of this passage, with its emphasis on repentance, on the one side, and the power of Israel to reform itself, on the other. The Messiah will come any day that Israel makes it possible. If all Israel will keep a single Sabbath in the proper (rabbinic) way, the Messiah will come. If all Israel will repent for one day, the Messiah will come. "Whenever you want...," the Messiah will come. Now, two things are happening here. First, the system of religious observance, including study of Torah, is explicitly invoked as having salvific power. Second, the persistent hope of the people for the coming of the Messiah is linked to the system of rabbinic observance and belief. In this way, the austere program of the Mishnah, with no trace of a promise that the Messiah will come if and when the system is fully realized, finds a new development. A teleology lacking all eschatological dimension here gives way to an explicitly messianic statement that the purpose of the law is to attain Israel's salvation: "If you want it, God wants it too." The one thing Israel commands is its own heart; the power it yet exercises is the power to repent. These suffice. The entire history of humanity will respond to Israel's will, to what happens in Israel's heart and soul. And, with Temple in ruins, repentance can take place only within the heart and mind.

A discussion of the power of repentance would hardly have surprised a Mishnah sage. What is new is at V-Z, the explicit linkage of keeping the law with achieving the end of time and the coming of the Messiah. That motif stands separate from the notions of righteousness and repentance, which surely did not require it. We must not lose sight of the importance of this passage, with its emphasis on repentance, on the one side, and the power of Israel to reform itself, on the other. The Messiah will come any day that Israel makes it possible. Let me underline the most important statement of this large conception: *If all Israel will keep a single Sabbath in the proper (rabbinic) way, the Messiah will come. If all Israel will repent for one day, the Messiah will come. "Whenever you want ...," the Messiah will come.*

Now, two things are happening here. First, the system of religious observance, including study of Torah, is explicitly invoked as having salvific power. Second, the persistent hope of the people for the coming of the Messiah is linked to the system of rabbinic observance and belief. In this way, the austere program of the Mishnah develops in a different direction, with no trace of a promise that the Messiah will come if and when the system is fully realized. Here a teleology lacking all eschatological dimension gives way to an explicitly messianic statement that the purpose of the law is to attain Israel's salvation: "If you want it, God wants it too." The one thing Israel commands is its own heart; the power it yet exercises is the power to repent. These suffice. The entire history of humanity will respond to Israel's will, to what happens in Israel's heart and soul. With the Temple in ruins, repentance can take place only within the heart and mind.

We should note, also, a corollary to the doctrine at hand, which carries to the second point of interest, the Messiah. Israel may contribute to its own salvation, by the right attitude and the right deed. But Israel bears responsibility for its present condition. So what Israel does makes history. Any account of the Messiah-doctrine of the Talmud of the Land of Israel must lay appropriate stress on that conviction: Israel makes its own history, therefore shapes its own destiny. This lesson, sages maintained, derives from the very condition of Israel even then, its suffering and its despair. How so? History taught moral lessons. Historical events entered into the construction of a teleology for the Talmud of the Land of Israel's system of Judaism as a whole. What the law demanded reflected the consequences of wrongful action on the part of Israel. So, again, Israel's own deeds defined the events of history. Rome's role, like Assyria's and Babylonia's, depended upon Israel's provoking divine wrath as it was executed by the great powers on earth.

VI. **THE STRUCTURE AND THE SYSTEM OF RABBINIC JUDAISM**

Looking backward from the end of the fourth century to the end of the first, the framers of the Talmud surely perceived what two hundred years earlier, with the closure of the Mishnah, need not have appeared obvious and unavoidable, namely, the definitive end, for here and now at any rate, of the old order of cultic sanctification. After a hundred years there may have been some doubt. After two centuries more with the fiasco of Julian near at hand, there can have been little hope left. The Mishnah had designed a world in which the Temple stood at the center, a society in which the priests presided at the top, and a way of life in which the dominant issue was the sanctification of Israelite life. Whether the full realization of that world, society, and way of life was thought to come sooner or later, the system had been meant only initially as a utopia, but in the end, as a plan and constitution for a material society here in the Land of Israel

Two hundred years now had passed from the closure of the Mishnah to the completion of the Talmud of the Land of Israel. Much had changed. Roman power had receded from part of the world. Pagan rule had given way to the sovereignty of Christian emperors. The old order was cracking; the new order was not yet established. But, from the perspective of Israel, the waiting went on. The interim from Temple to Temple was not differentiated. Whether conditions were less favorable or more favorable hardly made a difference. History stretched backward, to a point of disaster, and forward, to an unseen and incalculable time beyond the near horizon. Short of supernatural events, salvation was not in sight. Israel for its part lived under its own government, framed within the rules of sanctification, and constituted a holy society.

But when would salvation come, and how could people even now hasten its day? These issues, in the nature of things, proved more pressing as the decades rolled by, becoming first one century, then another, while none knew how many more, and how much more, must still be endured. So the unredeemed state of Israel and the world, the uncertain fate of the individual — these framed and defined the context in which all forms of Judaism necessarily took shape. The question of salvation presented each with a single ineluctable agendum. But it is not merely an axiom generated by our hindsight that makes it necessary to interpret all of a system's answers in the light of the single question of salvation. In the case of the Judaism to which the Talmud of the Land of Israel attests, the matter is explicitly stated.

For the important fact is that Talmud of the Land of Israel expressly links salvation to keeping the law. And, in the opposite way, so did Chrysostom. We recall that he held that not keeping the law showed that the Messiah had come and Israel's hope finally defeated. Sages maintained that keeping the law now signified keeping the faith: the act of hope. This means that the issues of the law were drawn upward into the highest realm of Israelite consciousness. Keeping the law in the right way is represented as not merely right or expedient. It is the way to bring the Messiah, the son of David. This is stated by Levi, as follows:

YERUSHALMI TAANIT 1:1.IX

X.   Said R. Levi, "If Israel would keep a single Sabbath in the proper way, forthwith the son of David would come.

Y.   "What is the Scriptural basis for this view? 'Moses said, Eat it today, for today is a Sabbath to the Lord; today you will not find it in the field' (Ex. 16:25)."

Z.   And it says, "For thus said the Lord God, the Holy One of Israel, 'In returning and rest you shall be saved; in quietness and in trust shall be your strength. And you would not' (Is. 30:15)."

Here, in a single saying, we find the entire Talmudic doctrine set forth. How like, yet how different from, the Mishnah's view. Keeping the law of the Torah represented the visible form of love of God.

The Mishnah's system, whole and complete, had remained reticent on the entire Messiah-theme. By contrast, our Talmud finds ample place for a rich collection of statements on the messianic theme. What this means is that, between the conclusion of the Mishnah and the closure of the Talmud, room had been found for the messianic hope, expressed in images not revised to conform to the definitive and distinctive traits of the Talmud itself. We do not have to argue that the stunning success of Christ (in the Christians' views) made the issue urgent for Jews. The issue had never lost its urgency, except in the tiny circle of philosophers who, in the system of the Mishnah, reduced the matter to a minor detail of taxonomy. And yet, in that exercise, the Mishnah's sages confronted a considerable social problem, one that faced the fourth century authorities as well.

The messianic hope in concrete political terms also required neutralization, so that peoples' hopes would not be raised prematurely, with consequent, incalculable damage to the defeated nation. That was true in the second century, in the aftermath of Bar Kokhba's war, and in the fourth century, for obvious reasons, as well. This "rabbinization" of the Messiah-theme meant, first of all, that rabbis insisted the Messiah would come in a process extending over a long period of time, thus not imposing a caesura upon the existence of the nation and disrupting its ordinary life. Accordingly, the Talmud of the Land of Israel treats the messianic hope as something gradual, to be worked toward, not a sudden cataclysmic event. That conception was fully in accord with the notion that the everyday deeds of people formed a pattern continuous with the salvific history of Israel.

YERUSHALMI YOMA 3:2.III.

A. Onetime R. Hiyya the Elder and R. Simeon b. Halapta were walking in the valley of Arabel at daybreak. They saw that the light of the morning star was breaking forth. Said R. Hiyya the Elder to R. Simeon b. Halapta, "Son of my master, this is what the redemption of Israel is like — at first, little by little, but in the end it will go along and burst into light.

B. "What is the Scriptural basis for this view? 'Rejoice not over me, O my enemy; when I fall, I shall rise; when I sit in darkness, the Lord will be a light to me' (Mic. 7:8).

C. "So, in the beginning, 'When the virgins were gathered together the second time, Mordecai was sitting at the king's gate' (Est. 2:19).

D. "But afterward: 'So Haman took the robes and the horse, and he arrayed Mordecai and made him ride through the open square of the city, proclaiming, Thus shall it be done to the man whom the king delights to honor' (Est. 6:11).

E. "And in the end: 'Then Mordecai went out from the presence of the king in royal robes of blue and white, with a great golden crown and a mantle of fine linen and purple, while the city of Susa shouted and rejoiced' [Est. 8:15].

F. "And finally: 'The Jews had light and gladness and joy and honor' (Est. 8:16)."

The pattern laid out here obviously does not conform to the actualities of the Christianization of the Roman Empire. From the viewpoint of Eusebius and Chrysostom alike, the matter had come suddenly, miraculously. Sages saw things differently. We may regard the emphasis upon the slow but steady advent of the Messiah's day as entirely consonant with the notion that the Messiah will come when Israel's condition warrants it. The improvement in standards of observing the Torah, therefore, to be effected by the nation's obedience to the clerks will serve as a guidepost on the road to redemption. The moral condition of the nation ultimately guarantees salvation. God will respond to Israel's regeneration, planning all the while to save the saved, that is, those who save themselves.

What is most interesting in Talmud of the Land of Israel's picture is that the hope for the Messiah's coming is further joined to the moral condition of each individual Israelite. Hence the messianic fulfillment was made to depend on the repentance of Israel. The entire drama, envisioned by others in earlier types of Judaism as a world-historical event, was reworked in context into a moment in the life of the individual and the people of Israel collectively. The coming of the Messiah depended not on historical action but on moral regeneration. So from a force that moved Israelites to take up weapons on the battlefield, the messianic hope and yearning were transformed into motives for spiritual regeneration and ethical behavior. The energies released in the messianic fervor were then linked to rabbinical government, through which Israel would form the godly society. When we reflect that the message, "If you want it, He too wants it to be," comes in a generation confronting a dreadful disappointment, its full weight and meaning become clear.

The advent of the Messiah will not be heralded by the actions of a pagan or of a Christian king. Whoever relies upon the salvation of a gentile is going to be disappointed. Israel's salvation depends wholly upon Israel itself. Two things follow. First, the Jews were made to take up the burden of guilt for their own sorry situation. But, second, they also gained not only responsibility for, but also power over, their fate. They could do something about salvation, just as their sins had brought about their tragedy. This old, familiar message, in no way particular to the Talmud's bureaucrats, took on specificity and concreteness in the context of the Talmud, which offered a rather detailed program for reform and regeneration. The message to a disappointed generation, attracted to the kin-faith, with its now-triumphant messianic fulfillment, and fearful of its own fate in an age of violent attacks upon the synagogue buildings and faithful alike, was stern. But it also promised strength to the weak and hope to the despairing. No one could be asked to believe that the Messiah would come very soon. The events of the day testified otherwise. So the counsel of the Talmud's sages was patience and consequential deeds. People could not hasten things, but they could do something. The duty of Israel, in the meantime, was to accept the sovereignty of heavenly government.

YERUSHALMI SANHEDRIN 6:9.III

A.   R. Abbahu was bereaved. One of his children had passed away from him. R. Jonah and R. Yosé went up [to comfort him]. When they called on him, out of reverence for him, they did not express to him a word of Torah. He said to them, "May the rabbis express a word of Torah."

B. They said to him, "Let our master teach us."

C. He said to them, "Now if on regard to the government below, in which there is no reliability, [but only] lying, deceit, favoritism, and bribe taking —

D. "which is here today and gone tomorrow —

E. "if concerning that government, it is said, **And the relatives of the felon come and inquire after the welfare of the judges and of the witnesses, as if to say, 'We have nothing against you, for you judged honestly' [M. San. 6:9],**

F. "on regard to the government above, in which there is reliability, but no lying, deceit, favoritism, or bribe taking —

G. "and which endures forever and to all eternity —

H. "all the more so are we obligated to accept upon ourselves the just decree [of that heavenly government]."

I. And it says, "That the Lord . . . may show you mercy, and have compassion on you . . . " (Deut. 13:17).

The heavenly government, revealed in the Torah, was embodied in this world by the figure of the sage. The meaning of the salvific doctrine just outlined becomes fully clear when we uncover the simple fact that the rule of Heaven and the learning and authority of the rabbi on earth turned out to be identified with one another.

It follows that salvation for Israel depended upon adherence to the sage and acceptance of his discipline. God's will in Heaven and the sage's words on earth — both constituted Torah. And Israel would be saved through Torah, so the sage was the savior — especially the humble one. The humblest of them all would be the sage-Messiah, victor over time and circumstance, savior of Israel. The sages of the Mishnah surely will have agreed, even though they would not have said, and did not say, things in quite this way. The structure of Rabbinic Judaism corresponds to its system; as things were, so they functioned. And so would they endure through all time to come.

II

The Character of
Pesiqta deRab Kahana

1. IDENTIFYING THE DOCUMENT

A compilation of twenty-eight propositional discourses, Pesiqta deRab Kahana (pisqa yields "chapter," so the plural can be rendered, "chapters attributed to R. Kahana), innovates because it appeals for its themes and lections to the liturgical calendar, rather than to a Pentateuchal book.[1] Pesiqta deRab Kahana marks a stunning innovation in Midrash-compilation because it abandons the pretense that fixed associative connections derive solely from Scripture. Rather, the document follows the synagogal lections. The text that governs the organization of Pesiqta deRab Kahana comprises a liturgical occasion of the synagogue, which is identical to a holy day, has told our authorship what topic it wishes to take up — and therefore also what verses of Scripture (if any) prove suitable to that topic and its exposition.

> *Adar-Nisan-Sivan*
> Passover-Pentecost: *Pisqaot* 2-12
> [possible exception: *Pisqa* 6]

---

[1] This chapter goes over the presentation of the document in my *Introduction to Rabbinic Literature*. N.Y., 1994: Doubleday. The Doubleday Anchor Reference Library For further reading see Bernard Mandelbaum, "Pesikta deRav Kahana," *Encyclopaedia Judaica* 13:333-334: the identification of the document, the original structure of the document and manuscript evidence, the manuscripts of the document; the original order followed the cycle of the Jewish calendar from the New Year through the Sabbath before the next New Year. My introduction is *Pesiqta deRab Kahana. An Analytical Translation and Explanation. II. 15-28. With an Introduction to Pesiqta deRab Kahana.* Atlanta, 1987: Scholars Press for Brown Judaic Studies. *From Tradition to Imitation. The Plan and Program of Pesiqta deRab Kahana and Pesiqta Rabbati.* Atlanta, 1987: Scholars Press for Brown Judaic Studies.

Tammuz-Ab-Elul
> The Ninth of Ab: *Pisqaot* 13-22

Tishré
> Tishré 1-22: *Pisqaot* 23-28

Only *Pisqa* 1 (possibly also *Pisqa* 6) falls out of synchronic relationship with a long sequence of special occasions in the synagogal lections. The twenty-eight parashiyyot of Pesiqta deRab Kahana in order follow the synagogal lections from early spring through fall, in the Western calendar, from late February or early March through late September or early October, approximately half of the solar year, 27 weeks, and somewhat more than half of the lunar year. On the very surface, the basic building block is the theme of a given lectionary Sabbath — that is, a Sabbath distinguished by a particular lection — and not the theme dictated by a given passage of Scripture, let alone the exposition of the language or proposition of such a scriptural verse. The topical program of the document may be defined very simply: expositions of themes dictated by special Sabbaths or festivals and their lections.

PISQA	BASE-VERSE
	TOPIC OR OCCASION

1.	*On the day Moses completed* (Num. 7:1)
	Torah-lection for the Sabbath of Hanukkah
2.	*When you take the census* (Ex. 30:12)
	Torah-lection for the Sabbath of Sheqalim
	first of the four Sabbaths prior to the advent
	of Nisan, in which Passover.falls
3.	*Remember Amalek* (Deut. 25:17-19)
	Torah-lection for the Sabbath of Zakhor
	second of the four Sabbaths prior to the advent
	of Nisan, in which Passover.falls
4.	*Red heifer* (Num. 19:1ff.)
	Torah-lection for the Sabbath of Parah
	third of the four Sabbaths prior to the advent
	of Nisan, in which Passover.falls
5.	*This month* (Ex. 12:1-2)
	Torah-lection for the Sabbath of Hahodesh
	fourth of the four Sabbaths prior to the advent
	of Nisan, in which Passover.falls
6.	*My offerings* (Num. 28:1-4)
	Torah-lection for the New Moon which falls on a weekday
7.	*It came to pass at midnight* (Ex. 12:29-32)
	Torah-lection for the first day of Passover

8.   *The first sheaf* (Lev. 23:11)
                    Torah-lection for the second day of Passover
                    on which the first sheaves of barley
                    were harvested and waved as an offering
9.   *When a bull or sheep or goat is born* (Lev. 22:26)
                    Lection for Passover
10.   *You shall set aside a tithe* (Deut. 14:22)
                    Torah-lection for Sabbath
                    during Passover in the Land of Israel
                    or for the eighth day of Passover
                    outside of the Land of Israel
11.   *When Pharaoh let the people go* (Ex. 13:17-18)
                    Torah-lection for the Seventh Day of Passover
12.   *In the third month* (Ex. 19:1ff.)
                    Torah-lection for Pentecost
13.   *The words of Jeremiah* (Jer. 1:1-3)
                    Prophetic lection for the first
                    of three Sabbaths prior to the Ninth of Ab
14.   *Hear* (Jer. 2:4-6)
                    Prophetic lection for the second
                    of three Sabbaths prior to the Ninth of Ab
15.   *How lonely sits the city* (Lam. 1:1-2)
                    Prophetic lection for the third
                    of three Sabbaths prior to the Ninth of Ab
16.   *Comfort* (Is. 40:1-2)
                    Prophetic lection for the first
                    of three Sabbaths following the Ninth of Ab
17.   *But Zion said* (Is. 49:14-16)
                    Prophetic lection for the second
                    of three Sabbaths following the Ninth of Ab
18.   *O afflicted one, storm tossed* (Is. 54:11-14)
                    Prophetic lection for the third
                    of three Sabbaths following the Ninth of Ab
19.   *I even I am he who comforts you* (Is. 51:12-15)
                    Prophetic lection for the fourth
                    of three Sabbaths following the Ninth of Ab
20.   *Sing aloud, O barren woman* (Is. 54:1ff.)
                    Prophetic lection for the fifth
                    of three Sabbaths following the Ninth of Ab
21.   *Arise, Shine* (Is. 60:1-3)
                    Prophetic lection for the sixth
                    of three Sabbaths following the Ninth of Ab

22.   *I will greatly rejoice in the Lord* (Is. 61:10-11)
                    Prophetic lection for the seventh
              of three Sabbaths following the Ninth of Ab

23.   *The New Year*
                    No base verse indicated.
              The theme is God's justice and judgment.

24.   *Return O Israel to the Lord your God* (Hos. 14:1-3)
                    Prophetic lection for the Sabbath of Repentance
              between New Year and Day of Atonement

25.   *Selihot*
              No base verse indicated. The theme is God's forgiveness.

26.   *After the death of the two sons of Aaron* (Lev. 16:1ff.)
                    Torah-lection for the Day of Atonement

27.   *And you shall take on the first day* (Lev. 23:39-43)
           Torah-lection for the first day of the Festival of Tabernacles

28.   *On the eighth day* (Num. 29:35-39)
                    Torah-lection for the
              Eighth Day of Solemn Assembly

This catalogue draws our attention to three eccentric *pisqaot,* distinguished by their failure to build discourse upon the base verse. These are No. 4, which may fairly claim that its topic, the red cow, occurs in exact verbal formulation in the verses at hand; No. 23, the New Year, and No. 25, *Selihot.* The last-named may or may not take an integral place in the structure of the whole. But the middle item, the New Year, on the very surface is essential to a structure that clearly wishes to follow the line of holy days onward through the Sabbath of Repentance, the Day of Atonement, the Festival of Tabernacles, and the Eighth Day of Solemn Assembly.

It follows that, unlike Genesis Rabbah and Leviticus Rabbah, the document focuses upon the life of the synagogue. Its framers set forth propositions in the manner of the authorship of Leviticus Rabbah. But these are framed by appeal not only to the rules governing the holy society, as in Leviticus Rabbah, but also to the principal events of Israel's history, celebrated in the worship of the synagogue. What we do not find in this Midrash-compilation is exposition of Pentateuchal or prophetic passages, verse by verse; the basis chosen by our authorship for organizing and setting forth its propositions is the character and theme of holy days and their special synagogue Torah-lections. That is, all of the selected base verses upon which the *parashiyyot* or chapters are built, Pentateuchal or prophetic, are identified with synagogal lections for specified holy days, special Sabbaths or festivals.

The contrast to the earlier compilations — this one is generally assigned to ca. 500 — is striking. The framers of Sifra and Sifré to Numbers and Sifré to Deuteronomy follow the verses of Scripture and attach to them whatever messages they wish to deliver. The authorship of Genesis Rabbah follows suit, though less narrowly guided by verses and more clearly interested in their broader themes. The framers of Leviticus Rabbah attached rather broad, discursive and syllogistic statements to verses of the book of Leviticus, but these verses do not follow in close sequence, one, then the next, as in Sifra and documents like it. That program of exposition of verses of Scripture read in or out of sequence, of organization of discourse in line with biblical books, parallel to the Tosefta's and Talmuds' authorships exposition of passages of the Mishnah, read in close sequence or otherwise, we see, defines what our authorship has not done. Pesiqta deRab Kahana has been assembled so as to exhibit a viewpoint, a purpose of its particular authorship, one quite distinctive, in its own context (if not in a single one of its propositions!) to its framers or collectors and arrangers.

2. EDITIONS AND TRANSLATIONS

The first translation of the document is William G. (Gershon Zev) Braude and Israel J. Kapstein, *Pesikta de-Rab Kahana. R. Kahana's Compilation of Discourses for Sabbaths and Festal Days* (Philadelphia, 1975: Jewish Publication Society of America). This writer's *Pesiqta deRab Kahana. An Analytical Translation and Explanation.* I. *1-14.* II. *15-28. With an Introduction to Pesiqta deRab Kahana* (Atlanta, 1987: Scholars Press for Brown Judaic Studies).is the second, and first analytical translation. It also is the only translation of the critical text by Bernard Mandelbaum, *Pesiqta deRav Kahana. According to an Oxford Manuscript. With Variants from All Known Manuscripts and Genizoth Fragments and Parallel Passages. With Commentary and Introduction* (N.Y., 1962: Jewish Theological Seminary of America).

3. RHETORIC

Following the model of Leviticus Rabbah, Pesiqta deRab Kahana consists of twenty-eight syllogisms, each presented in a cogent and systematic way by the twenty-eight pisqaot, respectively. Each pisqa or chapter (simply a different word for parashah, with the plurla, pesiqta) contains an implicit proposition, and that proposition may be stated in a simple way. It emerges from the intersection of an external verse with the base verse that recurs through the pisqa, and then is restated by the systematic dissection of the components of the base verse, each of which is shown to say the same thing as all the others.

A pisqa in Pesiqta deRab Kahana systematically presents a single syllogism, which is expressed through the contrast of an external verse with the base verse — hence, the base verse/intersecting verse form. In this form the implicit syllogism is stated through the intervention of an contrastive verse into the basic proposition established by the base verse,. The second type of material proceeds to the systematic exegesis of the components of the base verse on their own, hence through the Exegetical Form. There is a third form, a syllogistic list, familiar from the Mishnah and prior Midrash-compilations as well. The first two forms occur in the same sequence, because the former of the two serves to declare the implicit syllogism, and the latter, to locate that implicit syllogism in the base verse itself. The third will then be tacked on at the end. Otherwise it would disrupt the exposition of the implicit syllogism. All of these forms are familiar and require no further explanation.

4. LOGIC OF COHERENT DISCOURSE

The document as a whole appeals to the fixed associations defined by synagogal lections, in sequence. The individual compositions are syllogistic.

5. TOPICAL PROGRAM

These synagogal discourses, read in their entirety, form a coherent statement of three propositions:

[1] God loves Israel, that love is unconditional, and Israel's response to God must be obedience to the religious duties that God has assigned, which will produce merit. Israel's obedience to God is what will save Israel. That means doing the religious duties as required by the Torah, which is the mark of God's love for — and regeneration of — Israel. The tabernacle symbolizes the union of Israel and God. When Israel does what God asks above, Israel will prosper down below. If Israel remembers Amalek down below, God will remember Amalek up above and will wipe him out. A mark of Israel's loyalty to God is remembering Amalek. God does not require the animals that are sacrificed, since man could never match God's appetite, if that were the issue, but the savor pleases God [as a mark of Israel's loyalty and obedience]. The first sheaf returns to God God's fair share of the gifts that God bestows on Israel, and those who give it benefit, while those who hold it back suffer. Observing religious duties, typified by the rites of The Festival, brings a great reward of that merit that ultimately leads to redemption. God's ways are just, righteous and merciful, as shown by God's concern that the offspring remain with the mother for seven days. God's love for Israel is so intense that he wants to hold them back for an extra day after The Festival in order to spend more time with them, because, unlike the nations of the world, Israel knows how to please God. This is a mark of God's love for Israel.

[2] God is reasonable and when Israel has been punished, it is in accord with God's rules. God forgives penitent Israel and is abundant in mercy. Laughter is vain because it is mixed with grief. A wise person will not expect too much joy. But when people suffer, there ordinarily is a good reason for it. That is only one sign that God is reasonable and that God never did anything lawless and wrong to Israel or made unreasonable demands, and there was, therefore, no reason for Israel

to lose confidence in God or to abandon him. God punished Israel to be sure. But this was done with reason. Nothing happened to Israel of which God did not give fair warning in advance, and Israel's failure to heed the prophets brought about her fall. And God will forgive a faithful Israel. Even though the Israelites sinned by making the golden calf, God forgave them and raised them up. On the New Year, God executes justice, but the justice is tempered with mercy. The rites of the New Year bring about divine judgment and also forgiveness because of the merit of the fathers. Israel must repent and return to the Lord, who is merciful and will forgive them for their sins. The penitential season of the New Year and Day of Atonement is the right time for confession and penitence, and God is sure to accept penitence. By exercising his power of mercy, the already-merciful God grows still stronger in mercy.

[3] God will save Israel personally at a time and circumstance of his own choosing. Israel may know what the future redemption will be like, because of the redemption from Egypt. The paradox of the red cow, that what imparts uncleanness, namely touching the ashes of the red cow, produces cleanness, is part of God's ineffable wisdom, which man cannot fathom. Only God can know the precise moment of Israel's redemption. That is something man cannot find out on his own. But God will certainly fulfill the predictions of the prophets about Israel's coming redemption. The Exodus from Egypt is the paradigm of the coming redemption. Israel has lost Eden — but can come home, and, with God's help, will. God's unique power is shown through Israel's unique suffering. In God's own time, he will redeem Israel.

To develop this point, the authorship proceeds to further facts, worked out in its propositional discourses. The lunar calendar, particular to Israel, marks Israel as favored by God, for the new moon signals the coming of Israel's redemption, and the particular new moon that will mark the actual event is that of Nisan. When God chooses to redeem Israel, Israel's enemies will have no power to stop him, because God will force Israel's enemies to serve Israel, because of Israel's purity and loyalty to God. Israel's enemies are punished, and what they propose to do to Israel, God does to them. Both directly and through the prophets, God is the source of true comfort, which he will bring to Israel.

Israel thinks that God has forsaken them. But it is Israel who forsook God, God's love has never failed, and will never fail. Even though he has been angry, his mercy still is near and God has the power and will to save Israel. God has designated the godly for himself and has already promised to redeem them. He will assuredly do so. God personally is the one who will comfort Israel. While Israel says there is no comfort, in fact, God will comfort Israel. Zion/Israel is like a barren woman, but Zion will bring forth children, and Israel will be comforted. Both God and Israel will bring light to Zion, which will give light to the world. The rebuilding of Zion will be a source of joy for the entire world, not for Israel alone. God will rejoice in Israel, Israel in God, like bride and groom.

6. A SAMPLE PASSAGE

We consider the way in which this compilation treats Num. 7:1, which we have already read through the eyes of the authors of Sifré to Numbers, and which, in Chapter Seventeen, we shall examine from the perspective of the writers of Pesiqta Rabbati.

PISQA ONE

On the day that Moses completed the setting up of the Tabernacle, he anointed and consecrated it (Num. 7:1)

I:I

.1 A. *I have come back to my garden, my sister, my bride* (Song 5:1):

B. R. Azariah in the name of R. Simon said, "[The matter may be compared to the case of] a king who became angry at a noble woman and drove her out and expelled her from his palace. After some time he wanted to bring her back. She said, 'Let him renew in my behalf the earlier state of affairs, and then he may bring me back.'

C. "So in former times the Holy One, blessed be he, would receive offerings from on high, as it is said, *And the Lord smelled the sweet odor* (Gen. 8:21). But now he will accept them down below."

.2 A. *I have come back to my garden, my sister, my bride* (Song 5:1):

B. Said R. Hanina, "The Torah teaches you proper conduct,

C. "specifically, a groom should not go into the marriage canopy until the bride gives him permission to do so: *Let my beloved come into his garden* (Song 4:16), after which, *I have come back to my garden, my sister, my bride* (Song 5:1)."

.3 A. R. Tanhum, son-in-law of R. Eleazar b. Abina, in the name of R. Simeon b. Yosni: "What is written is not, 'I have come into the garden,' but rather, *I have come back to my garden.* That is, 'to my [Mandelbaum:] canopy.'

B. "That is to say, to the place in which the the principal [presence of God] had been located to begin with.

C. "The principal locale of God's presence had been among the lower creatures, in line with this verse: *And they heard the sound of the Lord God walking about* (Gen. 3:8)."

.4 A. [*And they heard the sound of the Lord God walking about* (Gen. 3:8):] Said R. Abba bar Kahana, "What is written is not merely 'going,' but 'walking about,' that is, 'walking away from.'"

B. *And man and his wife hid* (Gen. 3:8):

C. Said R. Aibu, "At that moment the first man's stature was cut down and diminished to one hundred cubits."

.5 A. Said R. Isaac, "It is written, *The righteous will inherit the earth* (Ps. 47:29). Where will the wicked be? Will they fly in the air?

B. "Rather, the sense of the clause, *they shall dwell thereon in eternity* is, 'they shall bring the presence of God to dwell on the earth.'"

.6 A. [Reverting to 3.C,] the principal locale of God's presence had been among the lower creatures, but when the first man sinned, it went up to the first firmament.

B. The generation of Enosh came along and sinned, and it went up from the first to the second.

C. The generation of the flood [came along and sinned], and it went up from the second to the third.

D. The generation of the dispersion [came along] and sinned, and it went up from the third to the fourth.

E. The Egyptians in the time of Abraham our father [came along] and sinned, and it went up from the fourth to the fifth.

F. The Sodomites [came along], and sinned, ...from the fifth to the sixth.

G. The Egyptians in the time of Moses...from the sixth to the seventh.

H. And, corresponding to them, seven righteous men came along and brought it back down to earth:

I. Abraham our father came along and acquired merit, and brought it down from the seventh to the sixth.

J. Isaac came along and acquired merit and brought it down from the sixth to the fifth.

K. Jacob came along and acquired merit and brought it down from the fifth to the fourth.

L. Levi came along and acquired merit and brought it down from the fourth to the third.

M. Kohath came along and acquired merit and brought it down from the third to the second.

N. Amram came along and acquired merit and brought it down from the second to the first.

O. Moses came along and acquired merit and brought it down to earth.

P. Therefore it is said, *On the day that Moses completed the setting up of the Tabernacle, he anointed and consecrated it* (Num. 7:1).

The selection of the intersecting verse, Song 5:1, rests on the appearance of the letters KLT, meaning, completed, but yielding also the word KLH, meaning, bride. The exegete wishes to make the point that in building the tabernacle, Moses has brought God down to earth, 6.P. This he accomplishes by bringing the theme of "garden, bride" together with the theme of the union of God and Israel. The parable at 1.B then is entirely apt, since it wishes to introduce the notion of God's having become angry with humanity but then reconciled through Israel in the sacrificial cult. 1.B then refers to the fall from grace, with Israel as the noble spouse who insists that the earlier state of affairs be restored. C then makes explicit precisely what is in mind, a very effective introduction to the whole. No. 2 pursues the exegesis of the intersecting verse, as does No. 3, the latter entirely apropos. Because of 3.C, Nos. 4 is tacked on; it continues the exegesis of the proof-text but has no bearing on the intersecting verse. But No. 5 does — at least in its proposition, if not in its selection of proof texts. No. 6 then brings us back to 3.C, citing the language of the prior component and then making the point of the whole quite explicit. Even with the obvious accretions at No. 4, 5, the whole hangs together and makes its point — the intersecting verse, Song 5:1, the base verse Num. 7:1 — in a cogent way.

I:II

.1 A.   *King Solomon made a pavilion for himself* (Song 3:9) [The New English Bible: *The palanquin which King Solomon had made for himself was of wood from Lebanon. Its poles he made of silver, its head-rest of gold; its seat was of purple stuff, and its lining was of leather*]:

B.   *Pavilion* refers to the tent of meeting.

C.   *King Solomon made a ...for himself:* he is the king to whom peace [*shalom/shelomoh*] belongs.

.2 A.   Said R. Judah bar Ilai, "[The matter may be compared to the case of] a king who had a little girl. Before she grew up and reached puberty, he would see her in the market place and chat with her, or in alleyways and chat with her. But when she grew up and reached puberty, he said, 'It is not fitting for the dignity of my daughter that I should talk with her in public. Make a pavilion for her, so that I may chat with her in the pavilion.'

B.   "So, to begin with: *When Israel was a child in Egypt, then in my love of him, I used to cry out* (Hos 11:1). In Egypt they saw me: *And I passed through the land of Israel* (Ex. 12:12). At the sea they saw me: *And Israel saw the great hand* (Ex. 14:31). At Sinai they saw me: *Face to face the Lord spoke with you* (Deut. 5:4).

C.   "But when they received the Torah, they became a fully-grown nation for me. So he said, 'It is not appropriate to the dignity of my children that I should speak with them in public. But make me a tabernacle, and I shall speak from the midst of the tabernacle.'

D.   "That is in line with this verse: *And when Moses entered the tent of the presence to speak with God, he heard the voice speaking from above the cover over the ark of the pact from between the two cherubim: the voice spoke to him* (Num. 7:89)."

.3 A.   [*The palanquin that King Solomon had made for himself was of wood from Lebanon. Its poles he made of silver, its head-rest of gold; its seat was of purple stuff, and its lining was of leather*] ...*was of wood from Lebanon. Make for the tabernacle planks of acacia-wood as uprights* (Ex. 26:15).

B.   *Its poles he made of silver: The hooks and bands on the posts shall be of silver (Ex. 27:10).*

C.   ...*its head-rest of gold: Overlay the planks with gold, make rings of gold on them to hold the bars* (Ex. 26:29).

D.   ...*its seat was of purple stuff: Make a veil of finely woven linen and violet, purple, and scarlet yarn* (Ex. 26:31).

E.   ...*and its lining was of leather:*

F.   R. Yudan says, "This refers to the merit accruing on account of the Torah and the righteous."

G.   R. Azariah in the name of R. Judah bar Simon says, "This refers to the Presence of God."

.4 A.   Said R. Aha bar Kahana, "It is written, *And there I shall meet with you* (Ex. 25:22),

B.   "to teach that even what is on the outside of the ark-cover is not empty of God's presence."

.5 A.   A gentile asked Rabban Gamaliel, saying to him, "On what account did the Holy One, blessed be he, reveal himself to Moses in a bush?"

B.   He said to him, "If he had revealed himself to him in a carob tree or a fig tree, what might you have said?

C.   "It is so as to indicate that there is no place in the earth that is empty of God's presence."

.6 A.   R. Joshua of Sikhnin in the name of R. Levi: "To what may the tent of meeting be compared?

B.   "To an ocean-side cave. The sea tide flows and engulfs the cave, which is filled by the sea, but the sea is not diminished.

C.   "So the tent of meeting is filled with the splendor of the presence of God."

D.   Therefore it is said, *On the day that Moses completed the setting up of the Tabernacle, he anointed and consecrated it* (Num. 7:1).

Seen by itself, No. 1 has no bearing upon the larger context, but it does provide a good exegesis of Song 3:9 in terms of the theme at hand, the tabernacle.

The point of No. 2 is that the purpose of the tabernacle was to make possible appropriate communication between a mature Israel and God. Then the two items are simply distinct workings of the theme of the tabernacle, one appealing to Song 3:9, the other, Num. 7:89.

I:III

.1 A.   [Continuing the exegesis of the successive verses of Song 3:9ff.] *Come out, daughters of Jerusalem, you daughters of Zion, come out and welcome King Solomon, wearing the crown with which his mother has crowned him, on his wedding day, on his day of joy* (Song 3:11) [Braude and Kapstein: *Go forth, O younglings whose name Zion indicates that you bear a sign*]:

B.   Sons who are marked [a play on the letters that stand for the word, *come out*] for me by the mark of circumcision, by not cutting the corners of the head [in line with Lev. 19:27], and by wearing show-fringes.

.2 A.   *[...and welcome] King Solomon:*

B.   The king to whom peace belongs.

.3 A.   Another interpretation: *and welcome King Solomon:*

B.   The King [meaning God] who brings peace through his deeds among his creatures.

C.   He caused the fire to make peace with our father Abraham, the sword with our father Isaac, the angel with our father Jacob.

D.   It is the king who brings peace among his creatures.

E.   Said R. Yohanan, "*Merciful dominion and fear are with him* (Job 25:2) [that is, are at peace with him]."

F.   Said R. Jacob of Kefar Hanan, "*Merciful dominion* refers to the angel Michael, and *fear* to the angel Gabriel.

G.   "*With him* means that they make peace with him and do not do injury to one another."

H.   Said R. Yohanan, "The sun has never laid eyes on the blemished part of the moon [the black side], nor does one star take precedence over another one, nor does a planet lay eyes on the one above it."

I.   Said Rabbi, "All of them traverse as it were a spiral staircase."

.4 A.   It is written, *Who lays the beams of your upper chambers in the waters, who makes the flaming fires your ministers* (Ps. 104:2-3):

B.   R. Simeon b. Yohai taught, "The firmament is of water, the stars of fire, and yet they dwell with one another and do not do injury to one another.

C.   "The firmament is of water and the angel is of fire, and yet they dwell with one another and do not do injury to one another."

D.   Said R. Abin, "It is not the end of the matter [that there is peace between] one angel and another. But even the angel himself is half fire and half water, and yet they make peace."

E.   The angel has five faces — *The angel's body was like beryl, his face as the appearance of lightning, his eyes as torches of fire, his arms and feet like in color to burnished brass, and the sound of his words like the sound of a roaring multitude* (Dan. 10:6) — [yet none does injury to the other].

.5 A.   *So there was hail and fire flashing continually amid the hail* (Ex. 9:24):

B.   R. Judah says, "There was a flask of hail filled with fire."

C.   R. Nehemiah said, "Fire and hail, mixed together."

D.   R. Hanin said, "In support of the position of R. Judah is the case of the pomegranate in the pulp of which seeds can be discerned."

E.   R. Hanin said, "As to R. Nehemiah's position, it is the case of a crystal lamp in which are equivalent volumes of water and oil, which together keep the flame of the wick burning above the water and the oil."

.6 A.   [*So there was hail and fire flashing continually amid the hail* (Ex. 9:24)]: What is the meaning of *flashing continually*?

B.   Said R. Judah bar Simon, "Each one is eager in its [B&K, p. 10:] determination to carry out their mission."

C.   Said R. Aha, "[The matter may be compared to the case of] a king, who had two tough legions, who competed with one another, but when the time to make war in behalf of the king came around, they made peace with one another.

D.   "So is the case with the fire and hail, they compete with one another, but when the time came to carry out the war of the Holy One, blessed be he, against the Egyptians, then:*So there was hail and fire flashing continually amid the hail* (Ex. 9:24) — one miracle within the other [more familiar one, namely, that the hail and fire worked together]."

.7 A.   [*Come out, daughters of Jerusalem, you daughters of Zion, come out and welcome King Solomon,*] *wearing the crown with which his mother has crowned him, on his wedding day,* [*on his day of joy*] (Song 3:11):

B.   Said R. Isaac, "We have reviewed the entire Scripture and have not found evidence that Bathsheba made a crown for her son, Solomon. This refers, rather, to the tent of meeting, which is crowned with blue and purple and scarlet."

.8 A.   Said R. Hunia, "R. Simeon b. Yohai asked R. Eleazar b. R. Yosé, 'Is it possible that you have heard. from your father what was the crown with which his mother crowned him?'

B. "He said to him, 'The matter may be compared to the case of a king who had a daughter, whom he loved even too much. He even went so far, in expressing his affection for her, as to call her, 'my sister.' He even went so far, in expressing his affection for her, as to call her, 'my mother.'

C. "'So at the outset, the Holy One, blessed be he, expressed his affection for Israel by calling them, 'my daughter:' *Hear, O daughter, and consider* (Ps. 45:11). Then he went so far, in expressing his affection for them, as to call them, 'my sister:' *My sister, my bride* (Song 5:1). Then he went so far, in expressing his affection for them, as to call them, 'my mother:' *Attend to me, O my people, and give ear to me, O my nation* (Is. 51:4). The letters that are read as "my nation" may also be read as 'my mother.'" [The distinction between the ayin-sound, a rough breathing, and the aleph-sound, no rough breathing, is thus obscured for exegetical purposes, so that it is as if the one letter, yielding my nation, were interchangeable with the other, producing my mother.]

D. "R. Simeon b. Yohai stood and kissed him on his brow.

E. "He said to him, 'Had I come only to hear this teaching, it would have been enough for me.'"

.9 A. R. Joshua of Sikhnin taught in the name of R. Levi: "When the Holy One, blessed be he, said to Moses, 'Make me a tabernacle,' Moses might have brought four poles and spread over them [skins to make] the tabernacle. This teaches, therefore, that the Holy One, blessed be he, showed Moses on high red fire, green fire, black fire, and white fire.

B. "He said to him, 'Make me a tabernacle.'

C. "Moses said to the Holy One, blessed be he, 'Lord of the ages, where am I going to get red fire, green fire, black fire, or white fire?'

D. "He said to him, '*After the pattern which is shown to you on the mountain* (Ex. 25:40).'"

.10 A. R. Berekhiah in the name of R. Levi: "[The matter may be compared to the case of] a king who appeared to his household clothed in a garment [B&K, p. 11] covered entirely with precious stones.

B. "He said to him, 'Make me one like this.'

C. "He said to him, 'My lord, O king, where am I going to get myself a garment made entirely of precious stones?'

D. "He said to him, 'You in accord with your raw materials and I in accord with my glory.'

E. "So said the Holy One, blessed be he, to Moses, 'Moses, if you make what belongs above down below, I shall leave my council up here and go down and reduce my Presence so as to be among you down there.'

F. "Just as up there: *seraphim are standing* (Is. 6:2), so down below: *boards of shittim-cedars are standing* (Ex. 26:15).

G. "Just as up there are stars, so down below are the clasps."

H. Said R. Hiyya bar Abba, "This teaches that the golden clasps in the tabernacle looked like the fixed stars of the firmament."

.11 A. *[Come out, daughters of Jerusalem, you daughters of Zion, come out and welcome King Solomon, wearing the crown with which his mother has crowned him,] on his wedding day, [on his day of joy]* (Song 3:11):

B. *...on his wedding day* [B&K, p. 12:] the day he entered the tent of meeting.

C. *...on his day of joy:*

D. this refers to the tent of meeting.

E. Another interpretation of the phrase, *on his wedding day, on his day of joy* (Song 3:11):

F. *...on his wedding day,* refers to the tent of meeting.

G. *...on his day of joy* refers to the building of the eternal house.

H. Therefore it is said, *On the day that Moses completed the setting up of the Tabernacle, he anointed and consecrated it* (Num. 7:1).

The exegesis of Song 3:11 now receives attention in its own terms, our point of departure having been forgotten. No. 1 simply provides a play on one of the words of the verse under study. Nos. 2-6 proceed to work on the problem of the name of the king, Solomon. We have a striking and fresh approach at Nos. 2-3: the reference is now to God as King, and the name, Solomon, then is interpreted as God's function as bringing peace both among his holy creatures, the patriarchs and the angels, and also among the elements of natural creation. Both topics are introduced and then, at Nos. 4-6, the latter is worked out. God keeps water and fire working together and to do his bidding, they do not injure one another. The proof-text, Ex. 9:24, then leads us in its own direction, but at No. 6 discourse returns to the main point. No. 7 moves us on to a fresh issue, namely, Solomon himself. And now we see the connection between the passage and our broader theme, the tabernacle. The Temple is now compared to a crown. No. 8 pursues the interpretation of the same clause. But the point of interest is the clause, not the theme under broader discussion, so what we have is simply a repertoire of exegeses of the cited verse. No. 9 carries forward the theme of making the tabernacle. It makes the point that Moses was to replicate the colors he had seen on high. I see no connection to the preceding. It is an essentially fresh initiative. No. 10 continues along that same line, now making yet another point, which is that the tabernacle on earth was comparable to the abode of God in heaven. No. 11 brings us back to our original verse. We take up a clause-by-clause interpretation of the matter. No. 11.H is an editorial subscript, with no connection to the foregoing except the rather general thematic one. But the original interest in working on the theme of the building of the tabernacle as Israel's wedding day to God is well expressed, beginning to end.

I:IV

.1 A. *Who has ever gone up to heaven and come down again? Who has cupped the wind in the hollow of his hands? Who has bound up the waters in the fold of his garment? Who has fixed the boundaries of the earth? What is his name or his son's name, if you know it?* (Prov. 30:4):

B. *...Who has ever gone up to heaven:* this refers to the Holy One, blessed be he, as it is written, *God has gone up to the sound of the trumpet* (Ps. 37:6).

C. *...and come down again: The Lord came down onto Mount Sinai* (Ex. 19:20).

D. *...Who has cupped the wind in the hollow of his hands: In whose hand is the soul of all the living* (Job 12:10).

E. *...Who has bound up the waters in the fold of his garment: He keeps the waters penned in dense cloud-masses* (Job 26:8).

F. *...Who has fixed the boundaries of the earth: ...who kills and brings to life* (1 Sam. 2:6).

G. *...What is his name:* his name is the Rock, his name is The Almighty, his name is The Lord of Hosts.

H. *or his son's name, if you know it: My son, my firstborn is Israel* (Ex. 4:22).

.2 A. Another interpretation of the verse, *Who has ever gone up to heaven:* Who is the one whose prayer goes up to heaven and brings down rain?

B. This is one who with his hands sets aside the tithes that he owes , who brings dew and rain into the world.

C. *Who has cupped the wind in the hollow of his hands? Who has bound up the waters in the fold of his garment? Who has fixed the boundaries of the earth?* Who is the one whose prayer does not go up to heaven and bring down rain?

D. This is one who with his hands does not set aside the tithes that he owes, who does not bring dew and rain into the world.

.3 A. Another interpretation of the verse, *Who has ever gone up to heaven* :

B.   This refers to Elijah, concerning whom it is written, *And Elijah went up in a whirlwind to heaven* (2 Kgs. 2:11).

C.   *...and come down again: Go down with him, do not be afraid* (2 Kgs. 1:16).

D.   *Who has cupped the wind in the hollow of his hands: Lord, God of Israel, before whom I stand* (1 Kgs. 17:1').

E.   *Who has bound up the waters in the fold of his garment: And Elijah took his mantle and wrapped it together and smote the waters and they were divided* (1 Kgs. 2:8).

F.   *Who has fixed the boundaries of the earth: And Elijah said, See your son lives* (1 Kgs. 17:23).

.4 A.   Another interpretation of the verse, *Who has ever gone up to heaven and come down again:*

B.   This refers to Moses, concerning whom it is written, *And Moses went up to God* (Ex. 19:3).

C.   *...and come down again: And Moses came down from the mountain* (Ex. 19:14).

D.   *Who has cupped the wind in the hollow of his hands: As soon as I have gone out of the city, I shall spread my hands out to the Lord* (Ex. 9:29).

E.   *Who has bound up the waters in the fold of his garment: The floods stood upright as a heap* (Ex. 15:8).

F.   *Who has fixed the boundaries of the earth:* this refers to the tent of meeting,as it is said, *On the day on which Moses completed setting up the tabernacle* (Num. 7:1) — for the entire world was set up with it.

.5 A.   R. Joshua b. Levi in the name of R. Simeon b. Yohai: "What is stated is not 'setting up the tabernacle [without the accusative particle, *et*],' but 'setting up + *the accusative particle* + the tabernacle,' [and since the inclusion of the accusative particle is taken to mean that the object is duplicated, we understand the sense to be that he set up a second tabernacle along with the first].

B.   "What was set up with it? It was the world that was set up with [the tabernacle, that is, the tabernacle represented the cosmos].

C.   "For until the tabernacle was set up, the world trembled, but after the tabernacle was set up, the world rested on firm foundations."

D.   Therefore it is said, *On the day that Moses completed the setting up of the Tabernacle, he anointed and consecrated it* (Num. 7:1).

The intersecting verse, Prov. 30:4, is systematically applied to God, to tithing, then Elijah, finally Moses, at which point the exposition comes to a fine editorial conclusion. I cannot imagine a more representative example of the intersecting verse-base verse exposition. No. 5 is tacked on because it provides a valuable complement to the point of No. 4.

I:V

.1 A.   Another interpretation of the verse: *On the day that Moses completed the setting up of the Tabernacle, he anointed and consecrated it* (Num. 7:1):

   B.   The letters translated as "completed" are so written that they be read "bridal," that is, on the day on which [Israel, the bride] entered the bridal canopy.

.2 A.   R. Eleazar and R. Samuel bar Nahmani:

   B.   R. Eleazar says, "*On the day that Moses completed* means on the day on which he left off setting up the tabernacle day by day."

   C.   It has been taught on Tannaite authority: Every day Moses would set up the tabernacle, and every morning he would make his offerings on it and then take it down. On the eighth day [to which reference is made in the verse, *On the day that Moses completed the setting up of the Tabernacle, he anointed and consecrated it*] he set it up but did not take it down again.

   D.   Said R. Zeira, "On the basis of this verse we learn the fact that an altar set up on the preceding night is invalid for the offering of sacrifices on the next day."

   E.   R. Samuel bar Nahmani says, "Even on the eighth day he set it up and took it apart again."

   F.   And how do we know about these dismantlings?

   G.   It is in line with what R. Zeira said, "*On the day that Moses completed* means on the day on which he left off setting up the tabernacle day by day."

.3 A.   R. Eleazar and R. Yohanan:

   B.   R. Eleazar said, "*On the day that Moses completed* means on the day on which demons ended their spell in the world.

   C.   "What is the scriptural basis for that view?

   D.   "*No evil thing will befall you, nor will any demon come near you* [B&K p. 15] *by reason of your tent* (Ps. 91:10) — on the day on which demons ended their spell in the world."

   E.   Said R. Yohanan, "What need do I have to derive the lesson from another passage? Let us learn it from the very passage in which the matter occurs: *May the Lord bless you and keep you* (Num. 6:24) — keep you from demons."

.4 A.   R. Yohanan and R. Simeon b. Laqish:

B. R. Yohanan said, *"On the day that Moses completed* means on the day on which hatred came to an end in the world. For before the tabernacle was set up, there was hatred and envy, competition, contention, and strife in the world. But once the tabernacle was set up, love, affection, comradeship, righteousness, and peace came into the world.

C. "What is the verse of scripture that so indicates?

D. *"Let me hear the words of the Lord, are they not words of peace, peace to his people and his loyal servants and to all who turn and trust in him? Deliverance is near to those who worship him, so that glory may dwell in our land. Love and fidelity have come together, justice and peace join hands* (Ps. 85:8-10).

E. Said R. Simeon b. Laqish, "What need do I have to derive the lesson from another passage? Let us learn it from the very passage in which the matter occurs: *and give you peace.*

.5 A. *[On the day that Moses completed] the setting up of the Tabernacle, [he anointed and consecrated it]:*

B. R. Joshua b. Levi in the name of R. Simeon b. Yohai: "What is stated is not 'setting up the tabernacle [without the accusative particle, *et*],' but 'setting up + *the accusative particle* + the tabernacle,' [and since the inclusion of the accusative particle is taken to mean that the object is duplicated, we understand the sense to be that he set up a second tabernacle along with the first].

C. "What was set up with it? It was the world that was set up with [the tabernacle, that is, the tabernacle represented the cosmos].

D. "For until the tabernacle was set up, the world trembled, but after the tabernacle was set up, the world rested on firm foundations."

We work our way through the clause, *on the day that Moses completed.* No. 1 goes over familiar ground. It is a valuable review of the point of stress, the meaning of the word *completed.* No. 2 refers to the claim that from day to day Moses would set up and take down the tent, until on the day at hand, he left it standing; so the "completed" bears the sense of ceasing to go through a former procedure. The word under study bears the further sense of "coming to an end," and therefore at Nos. 3, 4, we ask what came to an end when the tabernacle was set up. The matched units point to demons, on the one side, and hatred, on the other. No. 5 moves us along from the word KLT to the following set, *accusative + tabernacle.*

I:VI

.1 A.   *[On the day that Moses completed the setting up of the Tabernacle], he anointed and consecrated it:*

B.   Since it is written, *he anointed and consecrated it,* why does it also say, *he anointed them and consecrated them* (Num. 7:1)?

C.   R. Aibu said, "R. Tahalipa of Caesarea, and R. Simeon:

D.   "One of them said, 'After he had anointed each one, he then anointed all of them simultaneously.'

E.   "The other said, '*And he anointed them* refers to an anointing in this world and another anointing in the world to come.'"

.2 A.   Along these same lines: *You shall couple the tent together* (Ex. 26:11), *You shall couple the curtains* (Ex. 26:6):

B.   R. Judah and R. Levi, R. Tahalipa of Caesarea and R. Simeon b. Laqish:

C.   One of them said, "Once he had coupled them all together, he went back and coupled them one by one."

D.   The other said, "*You shall couple the curtains and it shall be one* meaning, one for measuring, one for anointing."

I:VII.

.1 A.   *The chief men of Israel, heads of families — that is, the chiefs of the tribes, [who had assisted in preparing the detailed lists] came forward and brought their offering before the Lord* (Num. 7:2):

B.   [(Following B&K, p. 16:) The word for *tribes* can mean *rods*, so we understand the meaning to be, they had exercised authority through rods] in Egypt.

C.   *...who had assisted in preparing the detailed lists:* the standards.

.2 A.   *...came forward and brought their offering before the Lord, six covered wagons [and twelve oxen, one wagon from every two chiefs and from each one an ox]* (Num. 7:2):

B.   The six corresponded to the six days of creation.

C.   The six corresponded to the six divisions of the Mishnah.

D.   The six corresponded to the six matriarchs: Sarah, Rebecca, Rachel, Leah, Bilhah, and Zilpah.

E.   Said R. Yohanan, "The six corresponded to the six religious duties that pertain to a king: *[1] He shall not have too many wives* (Deut. 17:17), *[2] He shall not have too many horses* (Deut. 17:16), *[3] He shall not have too much silver and gold* (Deut. 17:17), *[4] He shall not pervert justice, [5] show favor, or [6] take bribes* (Deut. 16:9)."

.3 A.   The six corresponded to the six steps of the throne. How so?

B.   When he goes up to take his seat on the first step, the herald goes forth and proclaims, *He shall not have too many wives* (Deut. 17:17).

C. When he goes up to take his seat on the second step, the herald goes forth and proclaims, *He shall not have too many horses* (Deut. 17:16).

D. When he goes up to take his seat on the third step, the herald goes forth and proclaims, *He shall not have too much silver and gold* (Deut. 17:17).

E. When he goes up to take his seat on the fourth step, the herald goes forth and proclaims, *He shall not pervert justice.*

F. When he goes up to take his seat on the fifth step, the herald goes forth and proclaims, *...or show favor.*

G. When he goes up to take his seat on the sixth, step, the herald goes forth and proclaims, *...or take bribes* (Deut. 16:9).

H. When he comes to take his seat on the seventh step, he says, "Know before whom you take your seat."

.4 A. *And the top of the throne was round behind* (1 Kgs. 10:19):

B. Said R. Aha, "It was like the throne of Moses."

C. *And there were arms on either side of the throne by the place of the seat* (1 Kgs. 10:19):

D. How so? There was a scepter of gold suspended from behind, with a dove on the top, and a crown of gold in the dove's mouth, and he [Moses]would sit under it on the Sabbath, and it would touch but not quite touch [I am not sure whether the "it" is the dove, scepter, crown, or what.]

.5 A. The six corresponded to the six firmaments.

B. But are they not seven?

C. Said R. Abia, "The one where the King dwells is royal property [not counted with what belongs to the world at large].

We proceed with the detailed exposition of the verse at hand. The focus of interest, after No. 1, is on the reason for bringing six wagons. The explanations, Nos. 2 (+3-4), 5, relate to the creation of the world, the Torah, the life of Israel, the religious duties of the king, and the universe above. The underlying motif, the tabernacle as the point at which the supernatural world of Israel meets the supernatural world of creation, is carried forward.

I:VIII

.1 A. [*...came forward and brought their offering before the Lord, six] covered [wagons and twelve oxen, one wagon from every two chiefs and from each one an ox]* (Num. 7:2):

B. The word for covered wagons may be read to yield these meanings:

C. like a lizard-skin [B&K, p. 17: "it signifies that the outer surface of the wagons' frames was as delicately reticulated as the skin of a lizard"];

D. [and the same word may be read to indicate that the wagons were] decorated, or fully equipped.

E. It has been taught in the name of R. Nehemiah, "They were like a bent bow."

.2 A. *...twelve oxen, one wagon from every two chiefs ...:*

B. This indicates that two chiefs would together bring one wagon, while each tribe gave an ox.

.3 A. *These they brought forward before the tabernacle* (Num. 7:3):

B. This teaches that they turned them into their monetary value and sold them to the congregation at large [so that everyone had a share in the donation].

.4 A. *And the Lord spoke to Moses and said, [Accept these from them: they shall be used for the service of the tent of the presence"]:* (Num. 7:45):

B. What is the meaning of the word, *and said*?

C. R. Hoshaia taught, "The Holy One, blessed be he, said to Moses, 'Go and say to Israel words of praise and consolation.'

D. "Moses was afraid, saying, 'But is it not possible that the holy spirit has abandoned me and come to rest on the chiefs?'

E. "The Holy One said to him, 'Moses, had I wanted them to bring their offering, I should have said to you to 'say to them,' [so instructing them to do so], but *Take — it is from them [at their own volition, not by my inspiration]* (Num. 7:5) is the language that means, they did it on their own volition [and have not received the holy spirit].'"

.5 A. And who gave them the good ideas [of making the gift]?

B. It was the tribe of Issachar who gave them the good idea, in line with this verse: *And of the children of Issachar came men who had understanding of the times* (1 Chr. 12:33).

C. What is the sense of *the times*?

D. R. Tanhuma said, "The ripe hour [*kairos*]."

E. R. Yosé bar Qisri said, "Intercalating the calendar."

F. *They had two hundred heads* (1 Chr. 12:33):

G. This refers to the two hundred heads of sanhedrins that were produced by the tribe of Issachar.

H. *And all of their brethren were subject to their orders* (1 Chr. 12:33):

I. This teaches that the law would accord with their rulings.

J.   They said to the community, "Is this tent of meeting which you are making going to fly in the air? Make wagons for it, which will bear it."

.6 A.   Moses was concerned, saying, "Is it possible that one of the wagons might break, or one of the oxen die, so that the offering of the chiefs might be invalid?"

B.   Said to Moses the Holy One, blessed be he, *"They shall be used for the service of the tent of the presence* (Num. 7:5).

C.   "To them has been given a long-term existence."

.7 A.   How long did they live?

B.   R. Yudan in the name of R. Samuel bar Nahman, R. Hunia in the name of Bar Qappara, *"In Gilgal they sacrificed the oxen* (Hos. 12:12)."

C.   And where did they offer them up?

D.   R. Abba bar Kahana said, "In Nob they offered them up."

E.   R. Abbahu said, "In Gibeon they offered them up."

F.   R. Hama bar Hanina said, "In the eternal house [of Jerusalem] they offered them up."

G.   Said R. Levi, "A verse of Scripture supporting the view of R. Hama bar Hanina: *Solomon offered a sacrifice of peace offerings, which he slaughtered for the Lord, twenty-two thousand oxen* (1 Kgs. 8:63)."

H.   It was taught in the name of R. Meir, "They endure even to now, and they never produced a stink, got old, or produced an invalidating blemish."

I.   Now that produces an argument *a fortiori*:

J.   If the oxen who cling to the work of the making of the tent of meeting were given an eternal existence, Israel, who cling to the Holy One, blessed be he, how much the more so!

K.   *And you who cling to the Lord your God are alive, all of you, this day* (Deut. 4:4).

The exegesis of the verse in its own terms leads us through the several phrases, Nos. 1, 2, 3. No. 4, continuing at No. 6, with an important complement at No. 5, goes on to its own interesting question. No. 7 serves No. 6 as No. 6 serves No. 5.

III

Comfort, comfort my people, says your God. Speak tenderly to Jerusalem and cry to her that her warfare is ended, that her iniquity is pardoned, that she has received from the Lord's hand double for all her sins. (Is. 40:1-2)

Pesiqta deRab Kahana
Pisqa Sixteen

XVI:I

.1 A. *Can mortal man be more righteous than God, or the creature purer than his maker? [If God mistrusts his own servants and finds his messengers at fault, how much more those that dwell in houses whose walls are clay, whose foundations are dust, which can be crushed like a bird's nest, or torn down between dawn and dark, how much more shall such men perish outright and unheeded, die without ever finding wisdom?]* (Job 4:17-20):

B. Now can there be a man more righteous than his creator?

C. But one's deeds purify a person.

D. Said the Holy One, blessed be He, "Boaz brings comfort, should I not bring comfort?"

.2 A. Boaz brings comfort: *Boaz answered, It has certainly been told to me [all that you have done for your mother-in-law since your husband's death, how you left your father and mother, and the*

51

land of your birth and came to a people you did not know before yesterday or the day before yesterday. The Lord reward your deed; may the Lord the God of Israel, under whose wings you have come to take refuge, give you all that you deserve] (Ruth 2:11-12).

B.   Why is the verb for *tell* repeated two times? ["Certainly been told" is a translation of the Hebrew repetition the verb *told* twice for emphasis.]

C.   He said to her, "It has been told to me in the household, and it has been told to me in the field."

D.   *...all that you have done for your mother-in-law since your husband's death:* and it goes without saying, during the lifetime of your husband.

E.   *...how you left your father and mother:* your actual parents.

F.   *...and the land of your birth:* this refers to your neighborhood.

.3 A. Another interpretation: *...how you left your father and mother:* this refers to your idolatry: *...saying to a piece of wood, You are my father, and to stone, You have given birth to me* (Jer. 2:27).

B.   *...and the land of your birth:* this refers to your town.

.4 A. *...and came to a people you did not know before yesterday or the day before yesterday:*

B.   He said to her, "If you had come to us yesterday or the day before yesterday, we should not have accepted you, for the law governing the Amonites had not yet been renewed, prohibiting a male Ammonite, but not a female, a male Moabite but not a female."

.5 A. *The Lord reward your deed; [may the Lord the God of Israel, under whose wings you have come to take refuge, give you all that you deserve]:*

B.   He said to her, "He who is destined to pay a reward to the righteous will pay your reward."

C.   *...give you all that you deserve:*

D.   What is written for the sense, *all that you deserve*, is spelled to be read *Solomon.*

E.   Said R. Yose, "He said to her, Solomon will descend from you."

.6 A. *...May the Lord the God of Israel, under whose wings you have come to take refuge:*

B.   Said R. Abun, "The earth has wings, the dawn has wings, the sun has wings, the cherubs have wings, the heavenly creatures have wings, the seraphim have wings.

C.   "The earth has wings: *From the wing of the earth we have heard songs* (Is. 24:16).

D.   "...the dawn has wings: *I went up on the wings of dawn* (Ps. 139:9).

E. "...the sun has wings: *But to you who fear my name shall the sun of righteousness arise with healing in its wings* (Mal. 3:20).

F. "...the cherubs have wings: *And the sound of the wings of the cherubim* (Ez. 10:5).

G. "...the heavenly creatures have wings: *The noise of the wings of the living creatures* (Ez. 3:13).

H. "...the seraphim have wings: *Above him stood the seraphim. Each one of them had six wings* (Is. 6:2)."

I. Said R. Abun, "Great is the power of those who deal mercifully, for they take shelter not in shadow of the wings of the earth nor in the shadow of the wings of the dawn, nor in the shadow of the wings of the sun, nor in the shadow of the wings of the cherubs, nor in the shadow of the wings of the heavenly creatures, nor in the shadow of the wings of the seraphim.

J. "In the shadow of whom do they take refuge? In the shadow of the Holy One, blessed be He, as it is written, *Precious is the lovingkindness ordained by you O God. Because of it the children of men take refuge in the shadow of your wings* (Ps. 36:8)."

.7 A. She said, *"Indeed sir, you have eased my mind [and spoken kindly to me; may I ask you as a favor not to treat me only as one of your slave girls?" When meal-time came around,] Boaz said to her, "[Come here and have something to eat, and dip your bread into the sour wine." So she sat beside the reapers, and he passed her some roasted grain. She ate all she wanted and still had some left over]* (Ruth 2:13-14):

B. He said to her, 'Do not speak in such a way, that you have been counted among the slave girls, you are counted only among the matriarchs."

.8 A. [Reverting to 1.D: Said the Holy One, blessed be He, "Boaz brings comfort, should I not bring comfort?"] Lo, it is an argument a fortiori:

B. Now, if Boaz, who spoke words of goodness and comfort to the heart of Ruth, comforted her, when the Holy One, blessed be He, comes to comfort Jerusalem, how much the more so:

C. *Comfort, comfort my people,* says your God. *[Speak tenderly to Jerusalem and cry to her that her warfare is ended, that her iniquity is pardoned, that she has received from the Lord's hand double for all her sins]* (Is. 40:1-2).

The interesting point of stress comes at the end, that God will be the one to comfort Jerusalem, as the base-verse says. The interesting question is how the intersecting-verse contributes, since it is not cited. But the answer is obvious: *Can mortal man be more righteous than God, or the creature purer than his maker?* If Boaz comforts Ruth, then God will surely comfort Jerusalem. The selection of Ruth, of course, is not difficult to explain. But the reference to Solomon, not David, is curious and should not be taken lightly. The systematic exegesis of the materials on Boaz and Ruth then form a critical element in framing the desired message. While, self-evidently, what we have is a compilation of materials on Ruth, the purposive character of the whole makes a strong impression.

XVI:II

.1 A.   *I said to my heart, I have amassed great wisdom, [more than all my predecessors on the throne in Jerusalem; My heart saw much wisdom and knowledge' So I applied my mind to understand wisdom and knowledge, madness and folly, and I came to see that this too is chasing the wind. For in much wisdom is much vexation, and the more a man knows, the more he has to suffer]* (Qoh. 1:15-18):

B.   On the basis of this verse they have said: the heart sees, the heart hears, the heart speaks, the heart knows, the heart stands, the heart falls, the heart goes, the heart cries out, the heart rejoices, the heart is comforted.

C.   ...the heart sees: *My heart saw much wisdom and knowledge.*

D.   ...the heart speaks: *I said to my heart.*

E.   ...the heart knows: *The heart knows its own bitterness* (Prov. 14:10).

F.   ...the heart hears: *You have given to your servant a listening heart* (1 Kgs. 3:9).

G.   ...the heart stands: *Will your heart stand? Will your hand be strong?* (Ez. 22:14).

H.   ...the heart falls: *Let a man's heart not fall on that account* (1 Sam. 17:32).

I.   ...the heart goes: *And he said to him, My heart has not gone* (2 Kgs. 5:26).

J.   ...the heart cries out: *Their heart cried out to the Lord* (Lam. 2:18).

K.   ...the heart rejoices: *Therefore my heart rejoices and my glory exults* (Ps. 16:9).

L.   ...the heart is comforted: *Comfort, comfort my people, says your God. Speak tenderly to the heart of Jerusalem [and cry to her that her warfare is ended, that her iniquity is pardoned, that she has received from the Lord's hand double for all her sins]* (Is. 40:1-2).

The intersecting-verse introduces the theme of the heart, but the composition does not then work on the base-verse. Rather, we have a thematic essay on the traits of the heart, leading up to the climactic conclusion, made possible by our base-verse. So what we have is a syllogism, bearing the facts supplied by the proof-texts, which does not make a point particular to either the intersecting- or the base-verse, but which makes its own point and then serves – rather admirably, I think – to amplify the meaning of the base-verse. It follows that the categories, intersecting- and base-verse, do not fit very exactly.

XVI:III

.1 A.   *How can I give testimony against you [New English Bible: cheer you], whose plight is like yours, daughter of Jerusalem? To what can I compare you [for your comfort, virgin daughter of Zion? For your wound gapes wide as the ocean, who can heal you? For your wound gapes wide as the ocean, who can heal you? The visions that your prophets saw for your were false and painted shams]* (Lam. 2:13-14):

B.   *How can I give testimony against you:* "How many prophets have I called to witness against you!"

C.   Rabbi says, "One prophet in the morning, and one prophet at dusk, in line with this verse of Scripture: *And the Lord gave testimony against Israel and against Judah by every prophet and seer* (2 Kgs. 17:13).

D.   "What is written is my prophets [that is, the plural or two]."

E.   And R. Nathan says, "There were two prophets in the morning and two prophets at dusk: *Early rising and sending* (Jer. 7:25), in the morning, and *early rising and sending* (Jer. 7:25) at dusk."

.2 A.   Another interpretation of the verse *How can I give testimony against you [New English Bible: cheer you], whose plight is like yours, daughter of Jerusalem? To what can I compare you [for your comfort, virgin daughter of Zion? For your wound gapes wide as the ocean, who can heal you?]* (Lam. 2:13):

B.   [Interpreting the letters for give testimony to mean adorn, we render:] How many adornments have I set on you.

C.   For said R. Johanan, "On the day on which the Holy One, blessed be He, came down to Sinai to give the Torah to Israel, with him came six hundred thousand ministering angels, and each one of them had a crown in his hand, to place on the head of an Israelite."

D.   R. Abba bar Kahana in the name of R. Yohanan: "There were one million two hundred thousand, one to put on the crown, the other to gird him with armor."

E.   R. Huna the Elder of Sepphoris said, "It was with [Braude and Kapstein, p. 290:] girdles of magistracy, in line with the following verse: *He unties the bond of kings and binds their lioins with a girdle* (Job. 12:18)."

.3 A.   Another interpretation of the verse *How can I give testimony against you [New English Bible: cheer you], [whose plight is like yours, daughter of Jerusalem? To what can I compare you [for your comfort, virgin daughter of Zion? For your wound gapes wide as the ocean, who can heal you?]* (Lam. 2:13):

B.   [Reading the letters of the word for *give testimony* as though they read the word for *booty*,] "How much booty have I given to you, the booty in Egypt, the booty at the sea, the booty of Sihon and Og, the booty of the thirty-one kings.

.4 A.   Another interpretation of the verse *How can I give testimony against you [New English Bible: cheer you], whose plight is like yours, daughter of Jerusalem? To what can I compare you [for your comfort, virgin daughter of Zion? For your wound gapes wide as the ocean, who can heal you?]* (Lam. 2:13):

B.   [Reading the letters of the word for *give testimony* as though they spelled out the word for *call a meeting*,] "In how many meetings did I meet with you: in the tent of meeting, in Gilgal, in Shiloh, in Nob, in Gibeon, in the eternal house in two [Temples]."

.5 A.   ...*To what can I compare you [for your comfort, virgin daughter of Zion? For your wound gapes wide as the ocean, who can heal you?]* (Lam. 2:13):

B.   "To what nation have I compared you? What nation have I redeemed with a mighty hand, and upon the enemies of which I have brought ten plagues?

C.   "For what nation have a split the sea? For what nation have a brought in the quail? What nation have I drawn near to myself at Mount Sinai and to what nation have I given my Torah?

D.   "What nation have I encompassed with clouds of glory?"

.6 A.   ...*whose plight is like yours, daughter of Jerusalem?* (Lam. 2:13):

B.   [The meaning of the allusion to the daughter of Jerusalem derives from letters of the word for Jerusalem, which yield the sense:] the daughter that is full of reverence and who makes her peace with me.

.7 A.   *To what can I compare you for your comfort, [virgin daughter of Zion? For your wound gapes wide as the ocean, who can heal you?]* (Lam. 2:13):

B.   For R. Jacob bar Abonah said, "[The sense of the word for

> compare derives from the letters that always form the word for,
> agree with, reach a unanimous judgment, hence,] 'When I come
> to one mind with you, then I shall comfort you.'"

.8 A.   *...virgin daughter of Zion... :*

B.   [Reading the letters for the word for Zion to yield, distinguished:] children who are distinguished for me by circumcision, refraining from hair-cutting in an improper manner [Lev. 19:27], wearing show-fringes.

.9 A.   *For your wound gapes wide as the ocean, who can heal you? The visions that your prophets saw for your were false and painted shams]* (Lam. 2:13):

B.   Said R. Hilpai, "He Who is destined to heal the wound of the sea is the one who will heal you."

C.   Said R. Joshua bar Nehemiah, "Him to Whom you have said at the sea, *Who is like unto you* (Ex. 15:11) is the One who will heal you."

D.   Said R. Abin, "*Who will heal you? The visions that your prophets saw for your were false and painted shams* (Lam. 2:14)."

E.   And rabbis say, "*Who will heal you? Your prophets.*"

The systematic exegesis of the verse at hand never brings us back to the base-verse at all. The verse is appropriately chosen as to theme, and that is why so much work is invested into the systematic exegesis of a powerful statement, given an equally strong message.

XVI:IV

.1 A.   *You have loved right and hated wrong; so God, your God, has anointed you above your fellows with oil, the token of joy* (Ps. 45:8):

B.   R. Azariah in the name of R. Aha interpreted the verse to speak of our father, Abraham: "You find that before the Holy One, blessed be He, brought the flood on the Sodomites, our father, Abraham, said before the Holy One, blessed be He, 'Lord of the ages, You have bound yourself by an oath not to bring a flood upon the world. What verse of Scripture indicates it? *These days recall for me the days of Noah, as I swore that the waters of Noah's flood should never again pour over the earth, [so now I swear to you never again to be angry with you or reproach you]* (Is. 54:9). True enough, you are not going to bring a flood of water, but you are going to bring a flood of fire. Are you now going to act deceitfully against the clear intent of that oath? [If so you will not carry out the oath!]

C.   *"'Far be it from you to do this thing, to kill the righteous like the wicked* (Gen. 18:25).' *Will not the judge of all the earth do justly?* (Gen. 18:25).

D.   "'If you want justice, there can be no world, and if a world is what you want, there can be no justice. Why are you holding the rope at both ends? You want your world and you want justice. If you don't give in a bit, the world can never stand.'

E.   "Said the Holy One, blessed be He, to him, *Abraham, you have loved righteousness and hated wickedness. [Therefore God, your God, has anointed you with the oil of gladness above your fellows]* (Ps. 45:8).

F.   *"You have loved righteousness:* You have loved to justify my creatures.

G.   *"...and hated wickedness:* You have hated finding them guilty.

H.   *"Therefore God, your God, has anointed you with the oil of gladness above your fellows.*

I.   "What is the meaning of *above your fellows?*

J.   "Said to him the Holy One, blessed be He, 'From Noah to you I have spoken with none of them except with you, with whom I speak first of all.'

K.   "This is in line with this verse: *After these things the word of the Lord came to Abram in a vision, saying* (Gen. 15:1)."

.2 A. R. Azariah in the name of R. Judah bar Simon interpreted the verse to speak of Isaiah:

B.   "Said Isaiah, 'I was strolling in my study house, and I heard the voice of the Lord, *saying, Whom shall I send? And who will go for us?* (Is. 6:8).

C.   "He said, 'I sent Amos, and they called him the stammerer.'"

D.   Said R. Phineas, "Why was he called Amos? Because [his tongue was heave-laden (*amus*)] and so he was a stammerer."

E.   They said, "The Holy One, blessed be He, dismissed his entire world and brought his Presence to rest only on this stammerer, him of the cut-off tongue."

F.   [Resuming discourse broken off at C:] "'When I sent Micah, they hit him on the cheek.' *They smite the judge of Israel with a rod upon the cheek* (Mic. 4:14).

G.   "Now: *whom shall I send, And who will go for us* (Is. 6:8)?'

H.   "Forthwith: *Here am I, send me* (Is. 6:8).

I.   "Said to him the Holy One, blessed be He, "Isaiah, my children are depraved, they are troublesome. If you agree to be humiliated and beaten up by my children, [you may go on my mission, but if not, you may not go on my mission].'

J.   "He said to him, 'I agree on that stipulation: *I gave my back to the smiters and my cheeks to them who pulled out the hair* (Is. 50:6).

K.   "[Isaiah continued,] 'But I am not worthy of going on a mission to your children.'

L.   "Said to him the Holy One, blessed be He, 'Isaiah, *You have loved righteousness [and hated wickedness. Therefore God, your God, has anointed you with the oil of gladness above your fellows]* (Ps. 45:8).

M.   "*'You have loved righteousness:* You have loved to justify my creatures.

N.   "*'...and hated wickedness:* You have hated finding them guilty.

O.   "*'Therefore God, your God, has anointed you with the oil of gladness above your fellows."*

P.   "What is the meaning of the phrase, *above your fellows?*

Q.   "Said to him the Holy One, blessed be He, 'By your life, in the case of all other prophets, they each received the power of prophecy from another prophet: *And they said, The spirit of Elijah rests on Elisha* (2 Kgs. 2:15). *And he took of the spirit that was upon him and put it on the seventy elders* (Num. 11:25).

R.   "'But you receive the gift of prophecy directly from the mouth of the Holy One, blessed be He: *The spirit of the Lord God is upon me, because [the Lord] has anointed me* (Is. 61:1).

S.   "'And not only so, but all the prophets prophecy prophecies without without repetition, but you will prophecy words of consolation that are repeated: *Arise, arise* (Is. 51:9). *Awake, awake* (Is. 51:17). *Rejoice, yes I will rejoice* (Is. 61:10). *I, even I am He [who comforts you]* (Is. 51:12).

T.   "*Comfort, comfort my people, [says your God. Speak tenderly to the heart of Jerusalem and cry to her that her warfare is ended, that her iniquity is pardoned, that she has received from the Lord's hand double for all her sins]* (Is. 40:1-2).'"

The more standard form of the intersecting-verse/base-verse construction sets the intersecting-verse at the head and leads us back to the base-verse. The first of the two identifications presents us with Abraham as the exemplification of our intersecting-verse, the second, to Isaiah, with the result that, at the end, the curious usage of the duplicated verb becomes a sign of divine favor.

XVI:V

.1 A.   *If only you were my own true brother that sucked [my mother's breasts, then if I found you outside I would kiss you and no man would despise me]* (Song 8:1):

B.   Like what sort of brother?

C.   As Cain was to Abel?

D.   Cain killed Abel.

E.   As Ishmael was to Isaac?

F.   Ishmael hated Isaac.

G.   As Esau was to Jacob?

H.   Esau hated Jacob.

I.   As were the brothers of Joseph to Joseph?

J.   The brothers of Joseph hated Joseph.

K.   But rather, as Joseph was to his brothers.

.2 A.   You find that after all the wicked things that his brothers did to him, what is written in his regard? *But Joseph said to them, "Fear not, for am I in the place of God? As for you, you meant evil against me, but God meant it for good, to bring it about that many people should be kept alive, as they are today. So do not fear; I will provide for you and your little ones." Thus he spoke to their heart and comforted them* (Gen. 50:19-21).

B.   Said R. Simlai, "He said to them, 'You are the head and I am the body. If the head goes its way, what good is the body?'"

.3 A.   Another matter: He said to them, "You are to be compared to the dust of the earth, to the wild beast of the field, and to the stars. Lo, will I go and make war with them?

B.   "If I can overcome them, lo, I can overcome you, and if not, then I cannot overcome you. [Gen. R. 100:9 adds: As with the dust of the earth, who can wipe out the dust of the earth? You have been compared to the wild beast of the field. As with the wild beast of the field, who can wipe out the wild beasts of the field? You have been compared to the stars. Who can wipe out the stars? Ten stars tried to destroy one star and could not overcome it. As to twelve tribes, how can I change the order of the world that one star can destroy twelve stars?]"

.4 A.   Another matter: He said, "Should I become my father's nemesis, with his fathering and with my burying the brothers?"

B.   Another matter: He said, "Should I become the nemesis of God, with God's blessing [my brothers] and my cutting down [my brothers]?"

.5 A.   Another matter: He said to them, "You form part of the order of the world: there are twelve hours by day and twelve by night, twelve months, twelve zodiacal planets, twelve tribes.

B.   "Can I then annul the good order of the world?"

.6 A.   Another matter: He said to them, "Before you came down here, the Egyptians treated me like a slave. Now that you have come down here, my birth as a free man has become known."

.7 A.   Another matter: He said to them, "If I kill you, the Egyptians will say 'He picked up a gaggle of boys and called them his brothers.

B.   "'You may know that that is the fact, for in the end he trumped up charges against them and killed them.'"

.8 A.   Another matter: He said to them, "If I call you, the Egyptians will say, 'If with his brother he does not keep the faith, is he going to keep the faith with us?'"

B.   Thus: *He spoke to their heart and comforted them* (Gen. 50:21).

.9 A.   Now the matter yields an argument *a fortiori:*

B.   if Joseph, who spoke mild words to the hearts of his brothers and thereby comforted them,

C.   when the Holy One, blessed be He, comes to comfort Jerusalem, how much the more so:

D.   *Comfort, comfort my people, [says your God. Speak tenderly to the heart of Jerusalem and cry to her that her warfare is ended, that her iniquity is pardoned, that she has received from the Lord's hand double for all her sins]* (Is. 40:1-2).

The expansion dwells on what Joseph said to reassure the brothers. No. 2 provides an important link to the eschatological salvation of Israel, so that the present scene prefigures Israel's future history. The route to the base-verse is straight and true.

XVI:VI

.1 A.   *All your lovers have forgotten you, they seek you not, for I have wounded you with the wound of an enemy* (Jer. 30:14).

B.   [Reading the letters *Job* slightly differently, we have] the wound of an enemy.

C.   In regard to Job it is written, *[While he was yet speaking there came another and said,] "The Chaldeans formed three companies [and made a raid upon the camels and took, them and slew the servants with the edge of the sword, and I alone have ascaped to tell you"]* (Job 1:17).

D.   In regard to Jerusalem, it is written, *The city has been given into the hands of the Chaldeans* (Jer. 32:24).

E.   In regard to Job it is written, *The fire of God fell from heaven* (Job 1:16).

F.   In regard to Jerusalem, it is written, *From heaven fire has been sent into my bones and it has come down* (Lam. 1:13).

G.   In regard to Job it is written, *And he took a potsherd with which to scrape himself [and sat among the ashes]* (Job 2:8).

H.   In regard to Jerusalem, it is written, *[The precious sons of Zion worth their weight in fine gold,] how they are reckoned as earthen pots, [the work of a potter's hands]* (Lam. 4:2).

I.   In regard to Job it is written, *And they sat with him on the ground seven days [and seven nights and no one spoke a word to him, for they saw that his suffering was very great]* (Job 2:13).

J.   In regard to Jerusalem, it is written, *The elders of the daughter of Zion sit on the ground in silence; [they have cast dust on their heads and put on sackcloth; the maidens of Jerusalem have bowed their heads to the ground]* (Lam. 2:10).

K.   In regard to Job it is written, *I have sewed sackcloth upon my skin [and have laid my strength in the dust]* (Job 16:15).

L.   In regard to Jerusalem, it is written, *...and put on sackcloth; [the maidens of Jerusalem have bowed their heads to the ground]* (Lam. 2:10).

M.   In regard to Job it is written, *...and have laid my strength in the dust* (Job 16:15).

N.   In regard to Jerusalem, it is written, *...they have cast dust on their heads [and put on sackcloth; the maidens of Jerusalem have bowed their heads to the ground]* (Lam. 2:10).

O.   In regard to Job it is written, *Have pity on me, have pity on me, O you my friends, [for the hand of God has touched me]* (Job 19:21).

P.   In regard to Jerusalem, it is written, *For I will show you no favor* (Jer. 16:13).

Q.   In regard to Job it is written, *...for the hand of God has touched me* (Job 19:21).

R.   In regard to Jerusalem, it is written, *that she has received from the Lord's hand double [for all her sins]* (Is. 40:2).

S.   Said R. Joshua bar Nehemiah, "Now if in the case of Job, who was smitten two fold, he gave him his compensation twofold, so Jerusalem will be comforted twofold: *Comfort, comfort my people, says your God. [Speak tenderly to the heart of Jerusalem and cry to her that her warfare is ended, that her iniquity is pardoned, that she has received from the Lord's hand double for all her sins]* (Is. 40:1-2)."

The systematic comparison is aiming at the concluding observation, which serves to draw meaning to the language of the base-verse.

XVI:VII

.1 A.   *Surely no shall put forth his hand to a ruinous heap, neither because of these things shall help come in one's calamity* (Job 30:24):

B.   Said R. Abbahu, The Holy One blessed be He does not smite a nation and then leave it desolate, but he brings calamity to one and comforts another, brings calamity to one and comforts the other [by indicating that the punishment meted out to the one has affected the other].

C.   "He brought a calamity to Assyria and thereby comforted Egypt: *Are you better than No-Ammon* (Nahum 3:8).

D.   "He brought a calamity on Egypt and comforted Assyria: *Behold, the Assyrian was a cedar in Lebanon* (Ez. 31:3)."

E.   Said R. Yose, "On what account did the Ten Tribes go into exile and only afterward the tribes of Judah and Benjamin? It was so that the one should draw comfort from [what had happened to] the other."

F.   Therefore: *Comfort, comfort my people, says your God. [Speak tenderly to the heart of Jerusalem and cry to her that her warfare is ended, that her iniquity is pardoned, that she has received from the Lord's hand double for all her sins]* (Is. 40:1-2).

The point about the suffering of the one serving as consolation for the punishment meted out to the other, proved in the opening lines, then applies to Israel: Judah and Benjamin draw comfort from the prior suffering of Israel. This seems to me rather far-fetched, but the passage contains no problems and makes its point quite clearly. Braude and Kapstein insert at the beginning of **XVI:VIII.1.A:** The disasters that befell Israel were of such a kind as to invite comfort from others who have likewise suffered disaster, but that reading is hardly to be imposed on the relationship of Egypt and Assyria.

XVI:VIII

.1 A.   *How will you comfort me through vanity, and as for your answers, there remains only faithlessness* (Job 21:34):

B.   Said R. Abba bar Kahana [on the meaning of the word translated as faithlessness], "Your words [of comfort and consolation, that Job's friends had provided him] require clarification."

C.   Rabbis say, "Your words contain contradictions." [We shall now have a long series of examples of how God's messages to the prophets contradict themselves.]

.2 A.   The Holy One said to the prophets, "Go and comfort Jerusalem."

B.   Hosea went to give comfort. He said to her [the city], "The Holy One, blessed be He, has sent me to you to bring you comfort."

C.   She said to him, "What do you have in hand."

D.   He said to her, *I will be as the dew to Israel* (Hos. 14:6).

E.   She said to him, "Yesterday, you said to me, *Ephraim is smitten, their root is dried up, they shall bear no fruit* (Hos. 9:16), and now you say this to me? Which shall we believe, the first statement or the second?"

.3 A.   Joel went to give comfort. He said to the city, "The Holy One, blessed be He, has sent me to you to bring you comfort."

C.   She said to him, "What do you have in hand."

D.   He said to her, *It shall come to pass in that day that the mountains shall drop down sweet wine and the hills shall flow with milk* (Joel 4:18).

E.   She said to him, "Yesterday, you said to me, *Awake you drunkards and weep, wail, you who drink wine, because of the sweet wine, for it is cut off from your mouth* (Joel 1:5), and now you say this to me? Which shall we believe, the first statement or the second?"

.4 A.   Amos went to give comfort. He said to the city, "The Holy One, blessed be He, has sent me to you to bring you comfort."

C.   She said to him, "What do you have in hand."

D.   He said to her, *On that day I will raise up the fallen tabernacle of David* (Amos 9:11).

E.   She said to him, "Yesterday, you said to me, *The virgin of Israel is fallen, she shall no more rise* (Amos 5:2), and now you say this to me? Which shall we believe, the first statement or the second?"

.5 A.   Micah went to give comfort. He said to the city, "The Holy One, blessed be He, has sent me to you to bring you comfort."

C.   She said to him, "What do you have in hand."

D.   He said to her, *Who is like God to you who pardons iniquity and passes by transgression* (Mic. 7:18).

E.   She said to him, "Yesterday, you said to me, *For the transgression of Jacob is all this and for the sins of the house of Israel* (Mic. 1:56), and now you say this to me? Which shall we believe, the first statement or the second?"

.6 A.   Nahum went to give comfort. He said to the city, "The Holy One, blessed be He, has sent me to you to bring you comfort."

C.   She said to him, "What do you have in hand."

D.   He said to her, *The wicked one shall no more pass through you, he is utterly cut off* (Nahum 2:1).

E.   She said to him, "Yesterday, you said to me, *Out of you came he forth who devises evil against the Lord, who counsels wickedness* (Nah. 1:11), and now you say this to me? Which shall we believe, the first statement or the second?"

.7 A.   Habakkuk went to give comfort. He said to the city, "The Holy One, blessed be He, has sent me to you to bring you comfort."

C.   She said to him, "What do you have in hand."

D.   He said to her, *You have come forth for the deliverance of your people, for the deliverance of your anointed* (Hab. 3:13).

E.   She said to him, "Yesterday, you said to me, *How long, O Lord, shall I cry and you will not hear, I cry to you of violence* (Hab. 1:22), and now you say this to me? Which shall we believe, the first statement or the second?"

.8 A.   Zephaniah went to give comfort. He said to the city, "The Holy One, blessed be He, has sent me to you to bring you comfort."

C.   She said to him, "What do you have in hand."

D.   He said to her, *It shall come to pass at that time that I will search Jerusalem with the lamps* (Zeph. 1:12).

E.   She said to him, "Yesterday, you said to me, *A day of darkness and gloominess a day of clouds and thick darkness* (Zeph. 1:15), and now you say this to me? Which shall we believe, the first statement or the second?"

.9 A.   Haggai went to give comfort. He said to the city, "The Holy One, blessed be He, has sent me to you to bring you comfort."

C.   She said to him, "What do you have in hand."

D.   He said to her, *Shall the seed ever again remain in the barn? Shall the vine, the fig tree, the pomegranate, and the olive tree ever again bear no fruit? Indeed not, from this day I will bless you* (Hag. 2:19).

E.   She said to him, "Yesterday, you said to me, *You sow much and bring in little* (Hag. 1:6), and now you say this to me? Which shall we believe, the first statement or the second?"

.10 A.   Zechariah went to give comfort. He said to the city, "The Holy One, blessed be He, has sent me to you to bring you comfort."

C.   She said to him, "What do you have in hand."

D.   He said to her, *I am very angry with the nations that are at ease* (Zech. 1:15).

E.   She said to him, "Yesterday, you said to me, *The Lord was very angry with your fathers* (Zech. 1:2), and now you say this to me? Which shall we believe, the first statement or the second?"

.11 A.   Malachi went to give comfort. He said to the city, "The Holy One, blessed be He, has sent me to you to bring you comfort."

C.   She said to him, "What do you have in hand."

D.   He said to her, *All the nations shall call you happy, for you shall be a happy land* (Mal. 3:12).

E.   She said to him, "Yesterday, you said to me, *I have no pleasure in you says the Lord of hosts* (Mal. 1:10), and now you say this to me? Which shall we believe, the first statement or the second?"

.12 A.   The prophets went to the Holy One, blessed be He, saying to him, "Lord of the ages, Jerusalem has not accepted the comfort [that we brought her]."

B.   Said to them the Holy One, blessed be He, "You and I together shall go and comfort her."

C.   Thus we say: *Comfort, comfort my people* but read the letters for *my people* as *with me.*

D.   Let the creatures of the upper world comfort her, let the creatures of the lower world comfort her.

E.   Let the living comfort her, let the dead comfort her.

F.   Comfort her in this world, comfort her in the world to come.

G.   Comfort her on account of the Ten Tribes, comfort her on account of the tribe of Judah and Benjamin.

H.   [Thus we must understand the statement, *Comfort, comfort my people, says your God. Speak tenderly to the heart of Jerusalem and cry to her that her warfare is ended, that her iniquity is pardoned, that she has received from the Lord's hand double for all her sins* (Is. 40:1-2) in this way:] *Comfort, comfort my people* but read the letters for *my people* as *with me.*

This sustained a remarkably powerful exercise in contrasting contradictory statements of the prophets yields, at the end, a stunning revision of the message of the base-verse: God and the angels and all beings assemble to comfort Jerusalem. I cannot point to an equivalently sustained and effective composition in this literature.

XVI:IX

.1 A.   With reference to the verse, *Comfort, comfort my people, [says your God. Speak tenderly to the heart of Jerusalem and cry to her that her warfare is ended, that her iniquity is pardoned, that she has received from the Lord's hand double for all her sins]* (Is. 40:1-2),] R. Abin made two statements.

B.   R. Abin said, "The matter may be compared to the case of a king who had a palace. His enemies invaded it and burned it. Who has to be comforted, the palace or the owner of the palace? Is it not the owner of the palace?

C.   "Thus said the Holy One, blessed be He, 'The house of the sanctuary is my house, as it is written, *On account of my house, which has been destroyed* (Hag. 1:9). Who then has to be comforted? Is it not I?'

D.   "So it follows: *Comfort, comfort my people,* means, Comfort me, comfort me, my people."

.2 A.   R. Abin made a second statement.

B. R. Abin said, "The matter may be compared to the case of a king who had a vineyard. His enemies invaded it and cut it down and laid it waste. Who has to be comforted, the vineyard or the owner of the vineyard? Is it not the owner of the palace?

C. "Thus said the Holy One, blessed be He, 'Israel is my vineyard, *For the vineyard of the Lord of hosts is the house of Israel* (Is. 5:7). Who then has to be comforted? Is it not I?'

D. "So it follows: *Comfort, comfort my people*, means, Comfort me, comfort me, my people."

.3 A. R. Berekhiah made two statements, one in his own name and one in the name of R. Levi.

B. R. Berekhiah said, "The matter may be compared to the case of a king who had a flock. Wolves invaded the flock and decimated it. Who has to be comforted, the flock or the owner of the flock? Is it not the owner of the flock?

C. "Thus said the Holy One, blessed be He, 'Israel is my flock: *And I put my flock, the flock of my pasture...* (Ez. 34:31). Who then has to be comforted? Is it not I?'

D. "So it follows: *Comfort, comfort my people*, means, Comfort me, comfort me, my people."

.4 A. R. Berekhiah made a statement in the name if R. Levi: The matter may be compared to the case of a king who had a vineyard and handed it over to a sharecropper.

B. "When the vineyard produced good wine, he would say, 'How good is the wine of my vineyard!; But when it produced bad wine, he would say, 'How bad is the wine of my sharecropper['s vineyard]!'

C. "That sharecropper said to him, 'My lord, O king, whether it is good or bad, it's yours!'

D. "So to begin with, the Holy One, blessed be He, said to Moses, *Now go, I shall send you to Pharaoh, and bring out my people, the children of Israel from Egypt* (Ex. 3:10).

E. "But when they committed that deed [of the golden calf], what is written? *Go, descend, for* your *people has corrupted...* (Ex. 32:7).

F. "Said Moses before the Holy One, blessed be He, 'Lord of the ages, when they sin, they are mine, but when they are guiltless, they are yours? Not so! Whether they sin or whether they are guiltless, they are yours.'

G. "For it is written, *And they are your people and your inheritance* (Deut. 9:29), *Do not destroy your people and your inheritance* (Deut. 9:26), *Why is the Lord angry with your people* (Ex. 32:11), 'why are you going to destroy your people?'"

H.   Said R. Simon, "[Moses] did not desist from speaking with love
       of them until [God] had called them, My people: *For the Lord
       regretted the evil which he had thought of doing to his people*
       (Ex. 32:14)."

The three parallel parables yield a climactic one at the end, which makes
the same point in a different, and still more effective way. The people is always *my
people*, as the base-verse says. That general observation is restated at the end not
as a parable but as an exercise in the juxtaposition of texts, a separate mode of
discourse.

XVI:X

.1 A.   *[Comfort, comfort my people,]* will *your God say. [Speak tenderly
        to the heart of Jerusalem and cry to her that her warfare is ended,
        that her iniquity is pardoned, that she has received from the Lord's
        hand double for all her sins]* (Is. 40:1-2):

B.   R. Hanina bar Pappa and R. Simeon:

C.   [Focusing on the future tense of the phrase, *Comfort, comfort
        my people,* will *your God say,*] R. Hanina bar Papa said, "The
        Israelites said to Isaiah, 'Our lord, Isaiah, is it possible that you
        have come to comfort only that generation in the days of which
        the house of the sanctuary was destroyed?'

D.   "He said to them, 'It is to all generations that I have come to
        bring comfort. What is said is not, *Your God* has *said*, but rather,
        Your God will say.'"

E.   Said R. Simon, "The Israelites said to Isaiah, ''Our lord, Isaiah,
        is it possible that all these things that you say you have made up
        on your own?'

F.   "He said to them, 'It is to all generations that I have come to
        bring comfort. What is said is not, *Your God* has *said*, but rather,
        Your God will say.'"

G.   Said R. Hinenah son of R. Abba, "In eight passages [Is. 1:11, 18,
        33:10, 40:1, 25, 41:21 (2x), 66:9 (Mandelbaum, p. 278n.)], it is
        written, *Your God will say*, matching the eight prophets who
        prophesied after the house of the sanctuary [was first destroyed]
        and these are they: Joel, Amos, Zephaniah, Haggai, Zechariah,
        Malachi, Ezekiel, and Jeremiah."

The point is clear as stated, with the stress on the future consolation of
Israel, as against the view that the rebuilding of the second Temple fulfilled the
prophetic promises and there would be no future consolation for Israel. The response
is at G, which repeats the point made through citing verses. The passage of course

is not particular to our base-verse at all. But it is located here as part of the systematic exegesis of the successive clauses of the base-verse.

XVI:XI

.1 A.   *[Comfort, comfort my people, says your God.] Speak tenderly to the heart of Jerusalem and declare to her [that her warfare is ended, that her iniquity is pardoned, that she has received from the Lord's hand double for all her sins]* (Is. 40:1-2).

B.   When they sinned with the head, they were smitten at the head, but they were comforted through the head.

C.   When they sinned with the head: *Let us make a head and let us return to Egypt* (Num. 14:4).

D.   ...they were smitten at the head: *The whole head is sick* (Is. 1:5).

E.   ...but they were comforted through the head: *Their king has passed before them and the Lord is at the head of them* (Mic. 2:13).

.2 A.   When they sinned with the eye, they were smitten at the eye, but they were comforted through the eye.

B.   When they sinned with the eye: *[The daughters of Zion...walk]...with wanton eyes* (Is. 3:16).

C.   ...they were smitten at the eye: *My eye, my eye runs down with water* (Lam. 1:16).

D.   ...but they were comforted through the eye: *For every eye shall see the Lord returning to Zion* (Is. 52:8).

.3 A.   When they sinned with the ear, they were smitten at the ear, but they were comforted through the ear.

B.   When they sinned with the ear: *They stopped up their ears so as not to hear* (Zech. 7:11).

C.   ...they were smitten at the ear: *Their ears shall be deaf* (Mic. 7:16).

D.   ...but they were comforted through the ear: *Your ears shall hear a word saying, [This is the way]* (Is. 30:21).

.4 A.   When they sinned with the nose [spelled *af,* which can also mean, *yet* or *also*] [Braude and Kapstein, p. 299, add: with obscene gestures], they were smitten at the nose, but they were comforted through the nose.

B.   When they sinned with the nose: *And lo, they put the branch to their noses* (Ez. 8:17).

C.   ...they were smitten at the word *af* [also]: *I also will do this to you* (Lev. 26:16).

D.   ...but they were comforted through the word *af* [now meaning *yet*]: *And yet for all that, when they are in the land of their enemies, I will not reject them* (Lev. 26:44).

.5 A.   When they sinned with the mouth, they were smitten at the mouth, but they were comforted through the mouth.

B.   When they sinned with the mouth: *Every mouth speaks wantonness* (Is. 9:16).

C.   ...they were smitten at the mouth: *[The Aramaeans and the Philistines] devour Israel with open mouth* (Is. 9:11).

D.   ...but they were comforted through the mouth: *Then was our mouth filled with laughter* (Ps. 126:2).

.6 A.   When they sinned with the tongue, they were smitten at the tongue, but they were comforted through the tongue.

B.   When they sinned with the tongue: *They bend their tongue, [their bow of falsehood]* (Jer. 9:2).

C.   ...they were smitten at the tongue: *The tongue of the sucking [child cleaves to the roof of his mouth for thirst]* (Lam. 4:4).

D.   ...but they were comforted through the tongue: *And our tongue with singing* (Ps. 126:2).

.7 A.   When they sinned with the heart, they were smitten at the heart, but they were comforted through the heart.

B.   When they sinned with the heart: *Yes, they made their hearts as a stubborn stone* (Zech. 7:12).

C.   ...they were smitten at the heart: *And the whole heart faints* (Is. 1:5).

D.   ...but they were comforted through the heart: *Speak to the heart of Jerusalem* (Is. 40:2).

.8 A.   When they sinned with the hand, they were smitten at the hand, but they were comforted through the hand.

B.   When they sinned with the hand: *Your hands are full of blood* (Is. 1:15).

C.   ...they were smitten at the hand: *The hands of women full of compassion have boiled their own children* (Lam. 4:10).

D.   ...but they were comforted through the hand: *The Lord will set his hand again the second time [to recover the remnant of his people]* (Is. 11:11).

.9 A.   When they sinned with the foot, they were smitten at the foot, but they were comforted through the foot.

B.   When they sinned with the foot: *The daughters of Zion...walk...making a tinkling with their feet* (Is. 3:16).

C.   ...they were smitten at the foot: *Your feet will stumble upon the dark mountains* (Jer. 13:16).

D.   ...but they were comforted through the foot: *How beautiful upon the mountains are the feet of the messenger of good tidings* (Is. 52:7).

.10 A. When they sinned with *this*, they were smitten at *this*, but they were comforted through *this*.

B. When they sinned with *this*: *[The people said...Go, make us a god], for as for* this *man Moses..., [we do not know what has become of him]* (Ex. 32:1).

C. ...they were smitten at *this*: *For* this *our heart is faint* (Lam. 5:17).

D. ...but they were comforted through *this*: *It shall be said in that day, Lo,* this *is our God* (Is. 25:9).

.11 A. When they sinned with *he*, they were smitten at *he*, but they were comforted through *he*.

B. When they sinned with *he*: *They have denied the Lord and said, It is not* he (Jer. 5:12).

C. ...they were smitten at *he*: *Therefore he has turned to be their enemy, and* he himself *fought against them* (Is. 63:10).

D. ...but they were comforted through *he*: *I even I am* he *who comforts you* (Is. 51:12).

.12 A. When they sinned with fire, they were smitten at fire, but they were comforted through fire.

B. When they sinned with fire: *The children gather wood and the fathers kindle fire* (Jer. 7:18).

C. ...they were smitten at fire: *For from on high he has sent fire into my bones* (Lam. 1:13).

D. ...but they were comforted through fire: *For I, says the Lord, will be for her a wall of fire round about* (Zech. 2:9).

.13 A. When they sinned in double measure, they were smitten in double measure, but they were comforted in double measure.

B. When they sinned in double measure: *Jerusalem has sinned a sin* (Lam. 1:8).

C. ...they were smitten in double measure: *that she has received from the Lord's hand double for all her sins* (Is. 40:2).

D. ...but they were comforted in double measure: *Comfort, comfort my people, says your God. [Speak tenderly to the heart of Jerusalem and cry to her that her warfare is ended, that her iniquity is pardoned, that she has received from the Lord's hand double for all her sins]* (Is. 40:1-2).

The massive exercise reaches its climax with our base-verse and systematically makes the one point that, however Israel sinned, Israel was punished in due measure and will be comforted in precisely the same measure.

IV

But Zion said, "The Lord has forsaken me, my Lord has forgotten me." "Can a woman forget her sucking child, that she should have no compassion on the son of her womb? Even these may forget, yet I will not forget you. Behold I have graven you on the palms of my hands; your walls are continually before me." (Isaiah 49:14-16)

Pesiqta deRab Kahana
Pisqa Seventeen

XVII:I

.1 A. *I call to my my song in the night. Thereupon I commune with my heart and have my spirit make diligent search. [Will the Lord reject us for evermore and never again show favor? Has his unfailing love now failed us utterly, must his promise time and again be unfulfilled? Has God forgotten to be gracious, has he in anger withheld his mercies? Has his right hand, I said, lost its grasp? Does it hang powerless, the arm of the Most High? But then O Lord I call to mind your deeds, I recall your wonderful acts in times by. I meditate upon your works and muse on all that you have done]* (Ps. 77:7-12):

B.   R. Aibu and R. Judah bar Simon:

C.   [Interpreting the letters that spell out *my song* as if they were read, *my triumph* (Mandelbaum),] R. Aibu said, "The community of Israel said before the Holy One, blessed be He, 'Lord of the ages, I remember the destruction that I wrecked on the kingdoms, in line with this verse: *...who has broken your enemies in your hand* (Gen. 14:20)."

D.   And R. Judah bar Simon said, "The community of Israel said before the Holy One, blessed be He, 'Lord of the ages, I remember the songs that I sang before you by night, as it is said, *...so let us sound the music of our praises all our life long in the house of the Lord* (Is. 38:20)."

.2 A.   *I call to my song in the night:*

B.   This refers to the night, the night of Pharaoh, that concerning which it is written, *And it came to pass at midnight* (Ex. 12:29).

C.   This refers to the night, the night of Gideon, that concerning which it is written, *And it came to pass on that night that the Lord said to him, Arise, go down into the camp, for I have given it into your hand* (Judges 7:9).

D.   This refers to the night, the night of Sennacherib, that concerning which it is written, *And it came to pass on that night that the angel of the Lord went forth and smote in the camp of Assyria one hundred eighty-five thousand* (2 Kgs. 19:35).

E.   This is a night, and that is a night: *Thereupon I commune with my heart and have my spirit make diligent search.*

.3 A.   I commune with my heart and it searches out my deeds and says, *Will the Lord reject us for evermore and never again show favor?*

B.   God forbid, He has not abandoned, nor will He abandon [Israel].

C.   *For the Lord will not abandon forever...* (Lam. 3:31).

.4 A.   *[Will the Lord reject us for evermore] and never again show favor?*

B.   "In the past You would [using the verb just now translated, *show favor]* appease others in my behalf.

C.   "Moses was angry and You appeased him in my behalf: *And he returned to the camp* (Ex. 33:11).

D.   "Elijah was angry and You appeased him in my behalf: *Go, return to your way toward the wilderness of Damascus* (1 Kgs. 19:15).

E.   And now not to appease nor to be appeased?

.5 A.   *Has his unfailing love now failed us utterly?*

B.   "*Has his unfailing love now failed us utterly,*" said R. Reuben, "is Greek, in line with the word in Greek for *let go.*"

.6 A.   *...must his promise time and again be unfulfilled:*

B. R. Hinena bar Papa and R. Simeon:

C. R. Hinena bar Papa said, "Has that matter concerning which you spoke to Moses at Sinai come to an end: *And I shall show favor to whom I show favor, and I shall show mercy to whom I show mercy* (Ex. 33:19)."

D. And R. Simon said, "Has [your promise] come to an end and ceased, and in line with what Jeremiah said, *For I have taken away my peace from this people, says the Lord, even mercy and compassion* (Jer. 16:5)?"

.7 A. *Has God forgotten to be gracious, has He in anger withheld his mercies?*

B. "Have you forgotten that you are gracious? *A gracious God, merciful, the Lord is long suffering* (Ex. 34:6).

.8 A. *Has God forgotten to be gracious:*

B. [Reading the letters for to be gracious as though they spelled out the word for camps, we interpret:] ob, Shilo, Gibeon, and the eternal house twice.

.9 A. *...has He in anger withheld his mercies?*

B. Even though He has been angry, His mercy is near:

C. *But Zion said, "The Lord has forsaken me, my Lord has forgotten me." ["Can a woman forget her sucking child, that she should have no compassion on the son of her womb? Even these may forget, yet I will not forget you. Behold I have graven you on the palms of my hands; your walls are continually before me"]* (Isaiah 49:14-16).

What we have is a systematic reading of the clauses of the intersecting-verse in line with the interest of the base-verse: has God forgotten Israel? The Psalmist is taken to press that same question, even though not all of the clauses before us pursue that theme singlemindedly.

XVII:II

.1 A. *Has his right hand, I said, lost its grasp? [Does it hang powerless, the arm of the Most High?]* :

B. Said R. Samuel bar Nahman, "It is because we did not seek your face in true repentance that *your right hand has lost its grasp.*"

C. Said R. Alexandri, "That oath that you made for us at Horeb has been profaned, with the result that *your right hand has lost its grasp.*"

D. Said R. Simon, "Have you ever heard someone say that the orb of the sun is sick and cannot go up and give sunshine or that the orb of the moon is sick and cannot go up and give moonlight?

E. "If his servants do not fall ill, is it possible He falls ill?"

F.   Said R. Isaac, "The matter may be compared to the case of a powerful soldier who was living in a city, and the citizens relied on him that when marauders would come, he would go forth and show himself to them, and they would forthwith flee.

G.   "But when marauders came, he said to them, 'My right arm is weak.'

H.   "But the Holy One, blessed be He, is not that way. But: *the hand of the Lord is not too short to afford salvation* (Is. 59:1).

I.   "But *it is your sins that have made a division between you and your God* (Is. 59:2)."

.2 A.   *Has his right hand, I said, lost its grasp? [Does it hang powerless, the arm of the Most High?] :*

B.   Said R. Simeon b. Laqish, '[Following Mandelbaum, p. 283:] If it is a matter of an ailment, there is hope, for in the end the sick person recovers, but if it is a matter of a change in the character of the right arm, there is no hope.'"

C.   That is the position of R. Simeon b. Laqish, for R. Simeon b. Laqish said, "*If it is rejection you did reject us irretrievably, but you are only very angry against us* (Lam. 5:22): If it is a matter of rejection, there is no hope, if it is a matter of mere anger, [that will pass and] there is hope. For one who is angry in the end is appeased."]

D.   *But Zion said, "The Lord has forsaken me, my Lord has forgotten me." ["Can a woman forget her sucking child, that she should have no compassion on the son of her womb? Even these may forget, yet I will not forget you. Behold I have graven you on the palms of my hands; your walls are continually before me."]* (Isaiah 49:14-16).

The interpretation of the further clauses of our intersecting-verse once more make the point that God does forgive and that anger does pass. The reading of the elements at No. 1 has the effect of saying that, in the end, God is in total command; tthen No. 2 proceeds to what is the important and climactic comment.

XVII:III

.1 A.   *Why should any living man complain, any mortal who has sinned? [Let us examine our ways and put them to the test and turn back to the Lord]* (Lam. 3:39-40):

B.   Said R. Abun bar Yudan, "*Why should any living man complain* for it is sufficient for a man that he is alive?"

C.   Said R. Berekhiah, "With the source of life that is mine in Your hand, *why should any living man complain?*"

D.   Said R. Levi, "Why should a man complain to the One who lives for all ages. But if one wants to make a complaint, then let it be a *mortal who has sinned* [*who* complains against his sinning]."

E.   Said R. Yudan, "Let him stand like a man and confess his sins and not complain."

.2 A.   [With reference to the verse, *Why should any living man complain, any mortal who has sinned? Let us examine our ways and put them to the test and turn back to the Lord* (Lam. 3:39-40)], Rabbi says, "Said the Holy One, blessed be He, 'They are malcontents, children of malcontents [always complaining].

B.   "'The first Man: I was busy trying to make a help-mate for him: *I shall make a help mate for him* (Gen. 2:18), but he kept complaining before Me: *The woman whom you set with me is the one who gave me...* (Gen. 3:12).

C.   "'So Jacob treated me that way. I was busy with his son, planning to make him king over Egypt: *And Joseph is the ruler of the land* (Gen. 42:6), and he complained before me, saying, *My way is hid from the Lord* (Is. 40:27).

D.   "'So his children treated me that way in the wilderness. I was busy with them choosing light bread for them, of the sort that kings eat, so that none of them should make a pig of himself and come down with diarrhea, while they complained before me, saying, *Our souls are fed up with this light bread* (Num. Num. 21:5).

E.   "'So Zion treats me. I am busy with her, trying to remove the kingdoms from the world. Did I not already get rid of Babylonia, Media, and Greece, and am I not going to get rid of this wicked kingdom? And yet she complains before me saying, "He has forsaken me, he has forgotten me."'

F.   *"But Zion said, The Lord has forsaken me, my Lord has forgotten me."* [*"Can a woman forget her sucking child, that she should have no compassion on the son of her womb? Even these may forget, yet I will not forget you. Behold I have graven you on the palms of my hands; your walls are continually before me"*] (Isaiah 49:14-16)."

     The intersecting-verse introduces the theme of complaining. No. 1's exposition of the sense of the passage points toward the important matter, which is the groundlessness of Israel's complaint to God. Israel must be patient. Now it has its life – so No. 1 – and if it wishes to complain, let the complaint be against its own sins. Then, No. 2, God will conclude the work in which even now he is engaged. I see the two components as remarkably cogent.

XVII:IV

.1 A.   *Then my anger shall be kindled against them in that day and I will forsake them, and I will hide my face from them and they shall be devoured and many evils and troubles shall come upon them* (Deut. 31:17):

   B.   Said R. Aha, "The burning anger of the Holy One, blessed be He, is for one day. Had they repented, that would have cooled it off."

   C.   Said R. Tanhum, "'I shall do to you as you have done.' They do and I do likewise.

   D.   "They do: *They have abandoned me and violated my covenant* (Deut. 31:17).

   E.   "...and I do likewise: *and I will forsake them, and I will hide my face from them and they shall be devoured and many evils [and troubles shall come upon them]* (Deut. 31:17)."

.2 A.   *Then my anger shall be kindled against them in that day:* in Babylonia.

   B.   *...and I will forsake them:* in Media.

   C.   *...and I will hide my face from them:* in Greece.

   D.   *and they shall be devoured [and many evils and troubles shall come upon them]:* in in Edom.

   E.   That is in line with this verse: *Behold the fourth beast....devoured and broke in pieces and stamped the residue with its feet* (Dan. 7:7).

.3 A.   *...and many evils and troubles shall come upon them* (Deut. 31:17):

   B.   This corresponds to the one hundred less two rebukes that are listed in the Torah.

.4 A.   *...saying, Have not these evils come upon us because our God is not among us* (Deut. 31:17):

   B.   "Had he been within me, this would not have come upon me. Had he been within me, I should not have gone into exile."

   C.   *But Zion said, ["The Lord has forsaken me, my Lord has forgotten me." "Can a woman forget her sucking child, that she should have no compassion on the son of her womb? Even these may forget, yet I will not forget you. Behold I have graven you on the palms of my hands; your walls are continually before me"]* (Isaiah 49:14-16).

The complaint of Isaiah is worked back into a statement of the cause, that is, God has forsaken me and forgotten me because of my forsaking and forgetting him. No. 1 introduces that general point, at A, and at B the same point is made explicit. No. 2 then draws us near the issue of the present, which is the rule of Edom/Rome. No. 3's interlude is followed by the explicit statement of No. 4 that Israel's condition comes about because of its own actions – but also that Israel's salvation rests with a faithful and loving God. By bringing God within, Israel can look forward to the restoration.

XVII:V

.1 A.   *If I forget you O Jerusalem, may my right hand forget its skill* (Ps. 137:5):

B.   Bar Qappara said, "[Because the fate of Jerusalem affects God, speaker in the cited verse, it follows that] 'My fate is in your hand and your fate is in my hand.'

C.   "My fate is in your hand: *And your heart will become arrogant, and you will forget the Lord your God* (Deut. 8:14).

D.   "...and your fate is in my hand: *If I forget you O Jerusalem, may my right hand forget its skill* (Ps. 137:5)."

.2 A.   R. Dosa says, "*If I forget you O Jerusalem, may my right hand forget* how to do miracles."

.3 A.   R. Azariah, R. Abbahu in the name of R. Simeon b. Laqish: "You find that when sins had brought it about and enemies came into Jerusalem, they took the heroes of Israel and tied their hands behind their backs.

B.   "Said the Holy One, blessed be He, It is written, *With him am I in distress* (Ps. 91:15). My children are in distress, and shall I remain in comfort? It is as though *He tied his right hand behind him on account of the enemy* (Job 2:3)."

.4 A.   "At the end he revealed to Daniel [the time of the end]: *And you, go to the end [time of redemption]* (Dan. 12:13).

B.   "He said to him, 'Is it to give a full accounting of myself?'

C.   "He said to him, *You shall rest* (Dan. 13:12).'

D.   "He said to him, 'Is it an eternal rest [or only until the resurrection of the dead]?'

E.   "He said to him, *And you will arise* (Dan. 13:12).'

F.   "He said to him, 'Lord of the ages, with whom? Will it be with the righteous or the wicked?'

G.   "He said to him, *...to your fate* (Dan. 13:12), with the righteous who are like you.'

H.   "He said to him, 'When?'

I.   "He said to him, *...at the end of days* (Dan. 13:12).

J.   "He said to him, 'Lord of the ages, At the end of days or at the end of the right arm['s being bound, that is, when God no longer forgets Jerusalem and regains the ability of his right arm] (YMYM/YMYN)?'

K.   "He said to him, 'At the end of the right arm['s being bound]. At the end of that right arm's being bound that is presently subjugated.'

L.   "Said the Holy One, blessed be He, I have set an end to [the binding of] my right arm, for so long as my children are subjugated, my right arm is bound. When I have redeemed my children, I shall also have redeemed my right arm.'

.5 A.   That is in line with what David said [in the translation of Braude and Kapstein, p. 309:], *That they may be delivered for the sake of your beloved or redeem them for your right hand's sake, answer me* (Ps. 60:7):

B.   Said David before the Holy One, blessed be He, "So long as Israel continues to enjoy merit, do it for them *for the sake of your beloved,* Abraham, Isaac, and Jacob.

C.   "But when Israel no longer continues to enjoy merit, do it *for your right hand's sake:*

D.   ...*for your right hand's sake, answer me* (Ps. 60:7).

.6 A.   [...*for your right hand's sake, answer me* (Ps. 60:7):] Said David before the Holy One, blessed be He, "Lord of the ages, why is it the case that whoever loves you wanders? Let them rest, as you have said, *Deliver us.*

B.   On this basis, the sages have included in the Sabbath liturgy the prayer that begins with the word, *Deliver us.*

.7 A.   [...*for your right hand's sake, answer me* (Ps. 60:7):] Said David before the Holy One, blessed be He, "Lord of the ages, why is it the case that whoever loves you is impoverished? Give them prosperity'.

B.   That is in line with this verse of Scripture: *He delivers the poor from his poverty* (Job 36:15).

.8 A.   [...*for your right hand's sake, answer me* (Ps. 60:7):] Said David before the Holy One, blessed be He, "Lord of the ages, why is it the case that whoever loves you is weak? Give them strength."

B.   That is in line with this verse of Scripture: *And your bones will he strengthen* (Is. 58:11).

.9 A.   R. Eleazar in the name of R. Yose bar Zimrah: "An echo is destined to ring on the tops of the hills, saying, *A song. Sing a new song to the Lord* (Ps. 96:1)."

B.   R. Levi in the name of R. Hama bar Hanina said, "An echo is destined to ring in the tents of the righteous, saying, *The voice of rejoicing and salvation in the tents of the righteous* (Ps. 118:15)."

.10 A. Said the Holy One, blessed be He, "My right hand is destined to do all these miracles for you, *But Zion said, ["The Lord has forsaken me, my Lord has forgotten me." "Can a woman forget her sucking child, that she should have no compassion on the son of her womb? Even these may forget, yet I will not forget you. Behold I have graven you on the palms of my hands; your walls are continually before me"]* (Isaiah 49:14-16)."

This rather intricate composition moves rather steadily to its conclusion, with the parts both autonomous and also carefully strung together to form an encompassing whole, the point of which is stated explicitly at No. 10. The intersecting-verse announces the theme: God's fate is bound up with that of Israel. That is then refined: if God forgets Israel, God can no longer use his right hand, No. 2. No. 3 goes over the propositions of Nos. 1, 2. The colloquy with Daniel, No. 4, is inserted because of L. The intersecting-verse has clearly drawn the compositor's attention to the passage on that account. Nos. 5-8 go over meanings to be imputed to the letters that spell the word for deliver. No. 9 sets the stage for No. 10. It would not have presented itself as the most likely candidate for use here, but it does serve. And then the conclusion, a strong and cogent end.

XVII:VI

.1 A.   *But Zion said, The Lord has forsaken me, [my Lord has forgotten me]:*

B.   [Commenting on the letters that spell the word for *forsaken*, which can yield the word for *strength*,] said the community of Israel before the Holy One, blessed be He, "Lord of the ages, have you forgotten that strength concerning which [your] children spoke at the sea: *The Lord is my strength and my song* (Ex. 15:2)."

.2 A.   Another matter: *But Zion said, The Lord has forsaken me, my Lord has forgotten me:*

B.   *[The Lord has forsaken me]* like the forgotten sheaf.

C.   That is in line with this verse: *For the poor person and the stranger you shall forsake it* (Lev. 19:10).

.3 A.   Another matter: *But Zion said, The Lord has forsaken me, my Lord has forgotten me:*

B.   "The Lord abandons me before the eyes of the nations of the world."

C.   R. Hanina interpreted the verse to speak in concrete terms of the daughters of Zion:

D.   *"...because the daughters of Zion are haughty and walk with outstretched necks, [glancing wantonly with their eyes, mincing along as they go, tinkling with their feet, the Lord will smite with a scab the heads of the daughters of Zion and the Lord will lay bare their secret parts]* (Is. 3:16-17):

B.   *"because the daughters of Zion are haughty:* walking about arrogantly.

C.   *"...and walk with outstretched necks:* when one of them would put on her jewerly, she would stretch her neck forward to show it off.

D.   *...glancing wantonly with their eyes:*

E.   R. Nissa of Caesarea said, "They would paint their eyes with red paint."

F.   R. Simeon b. Laqish said, "With red collyrium."

G.   *...mincing along as they go:* If one of them was tall, she would bring along two short ones, one to talk on one side, one on the other, so that she would appear to float above them. But if one of them was short, she would wear thick sandals, and she would bring along two shorter ones and walk between them, so that she would look taller.

H.   *...tinkling with their feet:* R. Abba bar Kahana said, "She would make the figure of a dragon with bells on her slippers."

I.   Rabbis say, "She would bring an eggshell and fill it with balsam, and put it under the heel of her sandal. She would see a bunch of boys, she would stamp on it and break the shell and the scent would exude from it and would run through them like the poison of a snake."

J.   The Holy One, blessed be He, would say to Jeremiah, "Jeremiah, what are these doing here? Let them go into exile from here."

K.   And Jeremiah would follow after them and say to them, "My daughters, repent before the enemy comes against you."

L.   But what would they say to Him? *"Let Him make haste, let Him speed His work, that we may see it; [let the purpose of the Holy One of Israel draw near and let it come that we may know it]* (Is. 519). A general will see me and take me for his wife, a hyparch will see me and take me for his wife, [Lev. R. **XVI:I.2.N** adds:] a commander will see me and take me and seat me on a chariot. *So let the purpose of the Holy One of Israel draw near, and let it come, that we may know it* (Is. 5:19), so that we may know whose opinion will be brought to reality, ours or His!"

M.   Now when sin brought it about that the enemy came, they made themselves up and came out before them like whores.

N.   A general saw one and took her as his wife and brought her up and seated her on his chariot, a hyparch saw one and took her as his wife and brought her up and seated her on his chariot.

O.   Said the Holy One, blessed be He, "Lo, this would appear to carry out [their expectation,[so will theirs come about and mine not come about?"

P. What did the Holy One, blessed be He, do to them?

Q. Said R. Eleazar, "He smote them with leprosy, in line with this verse: *the Lord will smite with a scab the heads of the daughters of Zion,* and the word for smite can mean only leprsoy, in line with this verse, *For a swelling, an eruption* [which uses the same letters as the word for smite] *or a spot* (Lev. 14:56)."

R. R. Dosa bar Hanina said, "He brought up swarms of lice upon their heads."

S. "R. Hiyya bar Abba said, "He made them into slave women used as beasts of burden."

T. What are beasts of burden? [In Aramaic:] slave women.

U. R. Berekhiah and Hilpo b. R. Zebod in the name of R. Yose: [What is the meaning of the word for smote with a scab? It is to flow. He protected their families, [word for *scab* is similar to word for family].

V. "...*so as to preserve the holy seed, so that the holy seed should not be diluted among the peoples of the earth* [cf. Ezra 9:2]."

W. Nonetheless, they did not repent.

Y. Said the Holy One, blessed be He, "I know that the nations of the world will not keep away from those who suffer from those afflicted with flux [Lev. 15:1-15] or with leprosy."

Z. What did the Holy One, blessed be He, therefore do to them?

AA. ...*and the Lord will lay bare their secret parts.*

BB. What is the meaning of *will lay bare their secret parts*?

CC. The Holy One, blessed be He, made a gesture to their "srings" and they flowed blood, which filled the chariot with blood.

DD. When one of them saw it, he speared the woman with his spear and laid her before his chariot and the chariot rolled over her and split her.

EE. And they said to one another, "Keep away from them, they are unclean."

FF. That is what the prophet said in accusing them: *Get out, unclean, men cried to them, Get out, get out, [do not touch yes, they fled away and wandered]* (Lam. 4:15).

.4 A. [Commenting on the words, *yes, they fled away and wandered*] R. Hinena bar Papa and R. Simon:

B. R. Hinena bar Papa said, "The Israelites were not exiled until they had condemned [which uses the same letters as the word for *fled away*] the Holy One, blessed be He.

C. R. Simon said, "The Israelites were not exiled until they had become antagonists of the Holy One, blessed be He."

The exegesis of the language of the base-verse continues with attention to the word for forsaken. Nos. 1, 2 provide brief statements. No. 3 invokes an enormous exposition of Is. 13:16-17 to make the point that God will humiliate Israel before the nations of the world, so spelling out the full meaning of the statement that the Lord has forsaken Israel. No. 4 is tacked on because it amplifies the language of the closing proof-text of No. 3.

XVII:VII

.1 A.   *Can a woman forget the child she has nursed* (Is. 49:15):

B.   Iqo said, "[Referring to the letters for the word for *child one has nursed*, which yield the word for *burnt-offering*, the verse means:] Can a woman forget her burnt-offering? Have you forgotten the offerings which we made before you?"

C.   R. Huna in the name of R. Aha: "Said the Holy One blessed be He, 'The good deeds I shall not forget, but the bad ones I shall forget.

D.   "'What you said to the calf: *These are your gods* (Ex. 32:4) [I shall forget].

E.   "'The good deeds I shall not forget: what you said before me at Sinai: *whatever the Lord has said we shall do and we shall hear* (Ex. 24:7)."

The amplification of the passage goes over several possible meanings.

XVII:VIII

.1 A.   Said R. Abbahu, "There were two things that Israel asked before the Holy One, blessed be He, and the prophets said to them, 'You have not asked properly.'

B.   "The Israelites asked, *Let him come to us as the rain, as the latter rain that waters the earth* (Hos. 6:3).

C.   "The prophets said to them, 'You have not asked properly. As to rain, wayfarers are bothered by it, roof-plasterers are bothered by it, wine-pressers and grain-threshers are bothered by it.

D.   "'But if you wish to ask, say it this way: *I shall be as dew to Israel, and she will blossom like a rose* (Hos. 14:6).'

E.   "The Israelites further asked, *Set me as a seal on your heart* (Song 8:6).

F.   "The prophets said to them, 'You have not asked properly. As to the heart, sometimes it is open, sometimes it is hidden.

G.   "'But if you wish to ask, say it this way: [To be] *a crown of beauty in the hand of the Lord and a royal diadem in the open hand of your God* (Is. 42:3).'"

H.   R. Simon bar Quy in the name of R. Yohanan: "Said to them the Holy One, blessed be He, 'Neither you nor your prophets have asked in the proper way.

I.   "'But if you wish to ask, say it this way: *Behold I have graven you on the palms of my hands; your walls are continually before me.* (Is. 49:16). Just as it is not possible for a person to forget the palms of his hands, so also *Even these may forget, yet I will not forget you* (Isaiah 49:14-16)."

The concluding exercise draws us on in the base-verse by reading one clause of that verse in light of the other. But the composition is syllogistic and not exegetical, in that it makes a point of its own, around which its discourse proves cogent, namely, there is a right way of asking for something. That syllogism then dominates, even though it leads to a powerful conclusion to our entire *pisqa*.

V

O afflicted one, storm-tossed [and not comforted], behold, I will set your stones in antimony, and lay your foundations with sapphires. I will make your pinnacles of agate, your gates of carbuncles, and all your wall of precious stones. All your sons shall be taught by the Lord, and great shall be the prosperity of your sons. In righteousness you shall be established; you shall be far from oppression, for you shall not fear; and from terror, for it shall not come near you.
(Is. 54:11-14)

Pesiqta de Rab Kahana
Pisqa Eighteen

XVIII:I

.1 A.   *O sons of a man, how long shall my honor suffer shame? [How long will you love vain words and seek after lies? But know that the Lord has set apart the faithful for himself; the Lord hears when I call to him]* (Ps. 4:2-3):

B.   The reference to sons of a man alludes to Doeg and Ahitophel.

C.   Why does Scripture refer to them as sons of a man?

D.   For they are the sons of Abraham, Isaac and Jacob.

E.   The word man refers only to our father, Abraham, as it is said: *And now, return the wife of the man, because he is a prophet* (Gen. 20:7).

F.   The word man refers only to our father, Isaac, as it is said: *Who is this man, who is going* (Gen. 24:65).

G.   The word man refers only to our father, Jacob, as it is said: *A simple man* (Gen. 25:27).

.2 A.   *...how long shall my honor suffer shame? [How long will you love vain words and seek after lies?]* (Ps. 4:3):

B.   Said David, "How long will you bring shame on my honor and call me merely, 'Son of Jesse:' *Why has the son of Jesse not come* (1 Sam. 20:27). *I saw the son of Jesse* (1 Sam. 16:18). *WIll the son of Jesse give everyone of you [fields]* (1 Sam. 22:7). Do I not have a name?'"

.3 A.   *...how long will you love vain words and seek after lies?]* (Ps. 4:3):

B.   ...pursuing after words of vanity: "[The Lord] has abandoned him, forgotten him, the kingdom will never again return to him."

.4 A.   *...and seek after lies?* (Ps. 4:3):

B.   "What are you thinking? Is it that because my kingdom has been taken away from me for a while, that it is forever?"

.5 A.   *But know that the Lord has set apart the godly for himself; [the Lord hears when I call to him]:*

B.   "He has already sent word to me through the prophet Nathan and said to me, *The Lord will indeed remove your sin and you will not die* (2 Sam. 13:14)."

.6 A.   Another interpretation of the verse *O sons of a man, how long will you love vain words and seek after lies? [But know that the Lord has set apart the faithful for himself; the Lord hears when I call to him]* (Ps. 4:2-3):

B.   *O sons of a man* refers to the nations of the world.

C.   And why does Scripture refer to them as sons of a man?

D.   For they come from the sons of Noah's sons, and the word for man refers only to Noah, as it is said, *And Noah was a righteous man* (Gen. 6:9).

.7 A.   *...how long shall my honor suffer shame* refers to the house of the sanctuary.

B.   The Holy One, blessed be He, says, "How long will you bring shame to the honor of my house, spitting at it, dirtying it, doing your transgressions in it?"

.8 A.   *...How long will you love vain words:*

B.   ...pursuing after words of vanity: "[The Lord] has abandoned it, forgotten it, the Presence of God will never again return to it."

.9 A.   *...and seek after lies? (Ps. 4:3):*

B.   "What are you thinking? Is it that because I removed my presence from it for a while, that it is forever?"

.10 A.   *But know that the Lord has set apart the faithful for himself; the Lord hears when I call to him:*

B.   "I have already sent word to him through the prophet Isaiah and I have said to [Jerusalem]: *O afflicted one, storm-tossed [and not comforted, behold, I will set your stones in antimony, and lay your foundations with sapphires. I will make your pinnacles of agate, your gates of carbuncles, and all your wall of precious stones. All your sons shall be taught by the Lord, and great shall be the prosperity of your sons. In righteousness you shall be established; you shall be far from oppression, for you shall not fear; and from terror, for it shall not come near you]* (Is. 54:11-14).

This perfectly matched set, with David set against his detractors, then the Temple and Jerusalem set against its detractors, reading each clause of the intersecting-verse in light of the message the framer wishes to deliver, is perfect in form and stunning in effect. I cannot imagine a more powerful way of linking the messiah-theme to the message at hand than having David's temporary removal from the throne compared to the temporary defeat of Jerusalem and the temporary destruction of the Temple.

XVIII:II

.1 A.   *O afflicted one:*

B.   Afflicted through impoverishment of righteous men, afflicted through impoverishment of words of Torah, afflicted through impoverishment of religious duties and good deeds.

.2 A.   *...storm-tossed:*

B.   Thrown about, a nation that the nations of the world have tossed around.

C.   That is in line with this verse of Scripture: *Remember, O Lord, concerning the children of Edom the day of Jerusalem* (Ps. 137:7).

.3 A.   *[Remember, O Lord, against the children of Edom, the day of Jerusalem the day they said, raze it, raze it* (Ps. 137:7)]:

B.   R. Abba bar Kahana said, "The meaning of the Hebrew word translated *raze it* follows the sense of the same word as it occurs in the following verse: *The broad walls of Babylon shall be utterly razed* (Jer. 51:58)."

C.   R. Levi said, "The meaning of the Hebrew word translated *raze it* should be rendered as *empty it, empty it,* for it follows the sense of the same word as it occurs in the following verse: *She hastened and emptied her pitcher into the trough* (Gen. 24:20)."

D.   In the view of R. Abba bar Kahana, who holds that the word means *raze it, raze it,* the sense is that they went down to the very foundations, to the base.

E.   In the view of R. Levi, who holds that the word means, *empty it out, empty it out,* the sense is that they cut away to the very foundations.

The word-for-word exegesis of the elements of the base-verse now begins, with a clarification of the word for afflicted in the sense of impoverished, poor. In what is Jerusalem poor? No. 3 goes over familiar ground.

XVIII:III

.1 A.   *...and not comforted:*

B.   Said R. Levi, "In any passage in which it is said, 'She had no...,' she eventually would have.

C.   *"And Sarai was barren, she had no child* (Gen. 11:30). *Will Sarah give suck to children* (Gen. 21:7). [Better: *And the Lord remembered Sarah* (Gen. 21:1)].

D.   *"And Peninah had children but Hannah had no children* (1 Sam. 1:2). *And the Lord visited Hannah and she conceived and she bore three sons* (1 Sam. 2:21).

E.   *"She is Zion, there is none who cares for her* (Jer. 30:17). *And a redeemer will come to Zion and to those who turn from transgression* (Is. 59:20)."

The same process continues, though in the present case, the syllogism takes precedence over the clarification of the element of the base-verse. That is to say, the passage has been composed in terms of its own interests and not to clarify our base-verse in particular. That fact is beyond doubt, since A refers to a verse that makes no appearance in the body of discourse at all.

XVIII:IV

.1 A.   *...behold, I will set your stones in stibium [antimony], [and lay your foundations with sapphires. I will make your pinnacles of agate, your gates of carbuncles, and all your wall of precious stones. All your sons shall be taught by the Lord, and great shall be the prosperity of your sons. In righteousness you shall be established; you shall be far from oppression, for you shall* *not fear; and from terror, for it shall not come near you]* (Is. 54:11-14).

B. That is black stibium, in line with this verse: With stibium she painted her eyes and then attired her head (2 Kgs. 9:34).

C. Three things have been stated with regard to stibium:

D. It makes the eyelashes grow.

E. It stops tears.

F. It gets rid of [the eye disease called] princess.

.2 A. *...and lay your foundations with sapphires:*

B. That is the equivalent in Greek of sapphires.

.3 A. R. Yudan and R. Phineas:

B. R. Yudan said, "Every row of stones that is destined to be set in Jerusalem should be as beautiful as sapphires."

C. Said R. Phineas, "Is it possible that sapphire is soft? [Certainly not.]"

.4 A. [Showing that sapphire is hard, not soft, is the following] story: A [merchant] went down to Rome to sell sapphires. The purchaser said to him, 'The deal is on the stipulation that I can test the stone."

B. He said to him, "On that very stipulation."

C. What did he do? He took it and put it on an anvil and hit it with a hammer.

D. The anvil split, the hammer was smashed, but the sapphire did not lose.

The clarification of the base-verse deals only with details and does not advance the argument. Nos. 3, 4 may be read as a unit, but the coherence of the two opinions in No. 3 escapes me.

XVIII:V

.1 A. *[I will set your stones in antimony, and lay your foundations with sapphires.] I will make your pinnacles of agate, [your gates of carbuncles, and all your wall of precious stones]:* (Isaiah 54:12)

B. R. Abba bar Kahana said, "Like this, like that. [The stibium just now mentioned and the agate will both be used, in alternative lines, stibium in one, sapphire in the other (Mandelbaum)]."

C. R. Levi said, "They will be bright red."

D. R. Joshua b. Levi said, "They will be bright red stones."

.2 A. R. Joshua stood with Elijah, of blessed memory. He said to him, "Will my lord not show me these stones [that are mentioned in the verse at hand]?"

B. He said to him, "Yes."

C.   Through a miracle he showed one to him.

D.   There was the case of a ship that was sailing in the Great Sea, and all the passengers were gentiles. But there was a single Jewish child on board.

E.   A terrible storm came upon the ship in the sea. Elijah appeared to the child, and said to him, "Go on a mission for me to R. Joshua b. Levi and show him stones of the sort at hand, and I shall save this ship on account of the merit that you will thereby attain."

F.   He said to him, "R. Joshua b. Levi is the greatest men of the generation, and he is not likely to believe me."

G.   He said to him, "Indeed, but he is very humble, and he will believe you. And when you show him these stones, do not show them to him in front of anyone, but lead him to a cave that is three miles from Lydda and show them to him there."

H.   Then a miracle was done and the ship emerged whole.

I.   That child went to R. Joshua and found him in session in the great court of Lydda. He said to him, "My lord, I have something private to say to you."

J.   R. Joshua b. Levi got up.

K.   Note the humility of R. Joshua b. Levi, who went after the lad for three miles and never asked him, "What do you want of me?"

L.   When they came to the cave, he said to him, "My lord, these are the stones [of the sort about which you asked Elijah]."

M.   When he saw them, he was startled by their light and dropped them to the ground, and they were buried.

.3 A.   *I will make your pinnacles of agate:*

B.   [This refers to] your walls.

C.   *...your gates of carbuncles:*

D.   R. Jeremiah in the name of R. Samuel bar Isaac: "The Holy One, blessed be He, is destined to make the eastern gate of the house of the sanctuary – it and both of its two lattices – out of a single pearl."

.4 A.   R. Yohanan was in session and giving an exposition in the great assembly hall in Sepphoris: "The Holy One, blessed be He, is destined to make the eastern gate of the house of the sanctuary – it and both of its two lattices – out of a single pearl."

B.   Present was a heretic, a sailor, who said, "We do not find a stone even as large as the egg of a dove, and yet this one makes such a statement in session!"

C.   When the man was sailing on the Great Sea, his ship sank in the sea, and he descended into the depths, and there he saw the ministering angels chipping away [at such a pearl], shaping and carving designs on it.

D. He said to them, "What is this?"

E. They said to him, "This is the eastern gate of the house of the sanctuary, it and both of its two lattices, made out of a single pearl."

F. On the spot a miracle was done for him and he got out in one piece.

G. The next year he came and found R. Yohanan in session and giving an exposition on the same topic: "The Holy One, blessed be He, is destined to make the eastern gate of the house of the sanctuary – it and both of its two lattices – out of a single pearl."

H. He said to him, "Old man, old man, whatever you can relate, relate, whatever praise you can devise, give. For had my own eyes not seen it, I should not have believed."

I. He said to him, "And had your own eyes not seen, you would not have believed the things that I have stated in the Torah?" He laid his eyes on him and gave him a piercing look, and the man forthwith turned into a heap of bones.

.5 A. There was the case of a pious man who was walking by the shore of the sea at Haifa and he was meditating in his heart, saying, "Is it possible that the Holy One, blessed be He, is destined to make the eastern gate of the house of the sanctuary – it and both of its two lattices – out of a single pearl?"

B. An echo forthwith sounded out, saying to him, "Were you not totally pious, the attribute of justice would have come to rest on that man. The whole of the world I have created in six days, as it is written, *In six days the Lord made the heaven and the earth* (Ex. 31:17). As to the eastern gate of the house of the sanctuary, therefore, is it then not possible for me to make it and its two lattices out of a single pearl? [Obviously I can create anything I want.]"

C. Forthwith the man sought mercy on himself and said before him, "Lord of the ages, even so, it was only in my heart that I meditated about the matter, but with my lips I did not bring it to expression."

D. On the spot a miracle was done for him, and the sea split open before him, and he saw he saw the ministering angels chipping away [at such a pearl], shaping and carving designs on it.

E. He said to them, "What is this?"

F. They said to him, "This is the eastern gate of the house of the sanctuary, it and both of its two lattices, made out of a single pearl."

The clarification of the sorts of stones to be used in the rebuilding of the Temple and of Jerusalem and of the language of the base-verse accounts for the materials at hand.

XVIII:VI

.1 A. *...and all your wall [border] of precious stones:*

 B. Said R. Benjamin b. Levi, "In the future the boundaries of Jerusalem will be marked out by precious stones and pearls. And all Israelites will come and take what they want [and meet all their needs with the proceeds].

 C. "For in this world Israelites mark out the boundaries of their fields with stones and hedges, but in the future that is coming they will mark them out with precious stones and pearls.

 D. "That is in line with this verse: *"...and all your wall [border] of precious stones."*

.2 A. Said R. Levi, "In the future the boundaries of Jerusalem will be marked for a circumference of twelve miles by eighteen miles by precious stones.

 B. "For in this world if someone owes a debt to his fellow, he says to him, 'Let us go to court.'

 C. "Sometimes the judge makes peace between them, sometimes he does not make peace between them.

 D. "Two parties rarely come out satisfied.

 E. "But in the future that is coming, if someone owes a debt to his fellow and the other says to him, 'Let us go to the king-messiah in Jerusalem, when they reach the borders of Jerusalem, they find them covered with precious stones and pearls. So the one takes two of them and says to the other, 'Do I owe you more than this?' And the other says, 'Not even this much! Let it be forgiven you, let it be released for you [and you do not owe more].'

 F. "That is in line with this verse of Scripture: *...and all your wall [border] of precious stones."*

.3A. *All your sons shall be taught by the Lord, and great shall be the peace [prosperity] of your sons. [In righteousness you shall be established; you shall be far from oppression, for you shall not fear; and from terror, for it shall not come near you]* (Is. 54:11-14):

 B. There are four statements of how great will be the peace [of the coming age]:

 C. *In his days the righteous shall flourish, and great peace, until the moon is no more* (Ps. 72:7)

D.   *Great peace will they have who love your Torah* (Ps. 119:165)

E.   *The humble shall inherit the earth and delight themselves in great peace* (Ps. 37:11).

F.   And this verse: *and great shall be the peace [prosperity] of your sons.*

The systematic exegesis of the base-verse concludes with a duplicated explanation of why the boundaries of Jerusalem will be marked by precious stones and then a further eschatological conclusion at No. 3.

VI

I, even I, am He who comforts you. Who are you that you are afraid of a man who dies, of the son of man who is made like grass, and have forgotten the Lord, your Maker, who stretched out the heavens and laid the foundations of the earth, and fear continually all the day because of the fury of the oppressor, when he sets himself to destroy? And where is the fury of the oppressor? He who is bowed down shall speedily be released; he shall die and go down to the Pit, neither shall his bread fail. For I am the Lord your God, who stirs up the sea so that its waves roar – the Lord of hosts is his name. I have put my words in your mouth and have covered you in the shadow of my hand that I may plant the heavens and lay the foundations of the earth, and say to Zion, you are my people.

(Isaiah 51:12-16)

Pesiqta de Rab Kahana
Pisqa Nineteen

XIX:I

.1 A.   *[You know what reproaches I bear, all my anguish is seen by you.] Reproach has broken my heart, my shame and my dishonor are past hope; I looked for consolation and received none, for comfort and did not find any* (Ps. 69:19-21):

B.   "The reproach that has broken us are the Ammonites and Moabites."

C.   You find that when sin had made it possible for the gentiles to enter Jerusalem, the Ammonites and Moabites came in with them.

D.   They came into the house of the holy of holies and took the cherubim and put them onto a bier and paraded them around the streets of Jerusalem, saying, "Did not the Israelites say, 'We do not worship idols'? See what they were doing."

E.   That is in line with this verse of Scripture: *Moab and Seir say, [Behold the house of Judah is like all the other nations]* (Ez. 25:8).

F.   What did they say? "Woe, woe, all of them are as one."

G.   From that time the Holy One, blessed be He, said, *I have heard the shame of Moab and the blaspheming of the children of Ammon, who have shamed my people, the children of Israel, and aggrandized their border...Therefore as I live, says the Lord of hosts, the God of Israel, surely Moab shall be as Sodom and the children of Amon as Gomorrah* (Zeph. 2:8-9).

.2 A.   *...shame:*

B.   the sense of the word is, upon me has come a powerful blow, which has drained my strength.

.3 A.   *I looked for consolation and received none, for comfort and did not find any* (Ps. 69:19-21):

B.   Said the Holy One, blessed be He, *I, even I, am he who comforts you [who are you that you are afraid of a man who dies, of the son of man who is made like grass, and have forgotten the Lord, your Maker, who stretched out the heavens and laid the foundations of the earth, and fear continually all the day because of the fury of the oppressor, when he sets himself to destroy? And where is the fury of the oppressor? He who is bowed down shall speedily be released;he shall die and go down to the Pit, neither shall his bread fail. For I am the Lord your God, who stirs up the sea so that its waves roar – the Lord of hosts is his name]* (Isaiah 51:12-15).

The intersecting-verse is well chosen, since it presents a dramatic contrast between the complaint, that there is no comfort, and God's statement that he is the one who brings comfort. The prior exposition of the intersecting-verse in terms of the Moabites bears its own relevance, since it sets the state for the catastrophe from which Israelite claims to derive no comfort. So the whole is cogent and the message exceedingly sharp.

XIX:II

.1 A. *Hear me when I groan, with no one to comfort me. [All my enemies, when they heard of my calamity, rejoiced at what you had done, but hasten the day you have promised when they shall become like me]* (Lam. 2:21):

B. R. Joshua of Sikhnin in the name of R. Levi interpreted the verse of Scripture to represent Aaron, the high priest:

C. "You find that when when Aaron, the high priest, died, the Canaanites came and made war against Israel, in line with the following verse of Scripture: *When the Canaanite, the king of Arad, who dwelled in the south, heard tell that Israel came by the way of Atarim* (Num. 21:1).

D. "What is the meaning of *by the way of Atarim*?

E. "It is that Aaron had died, the great pathfinder ["pathfinder" in Hebrew is similar to *Atarim*] of theirs, who explored the path for them.

F. *"...with no one to comfort me:*

G. "Moses was in mourning, Eleazar was in mourning. *All my enemies, when they heard of my calamity, rejoiced [at what you had done].*

H. "They said, 'It is time to go and come against them, it is time to go and destroy their enemies [that is, them].'"

.2 A. Rabbis interpreted the cited verse to speak of the nations of the world:

B. "You find that when the sins of Israel made it possible for the gentiles to enter Jerusalem, they made the decree that in every place to which they would flee, they should close [the gates before them].

C. "They tried to flee to the south, but they did not let them: *Thus says the Lord, for three transgressions of Gaza, yes for four, I will not reverse it [because they permitted an entire captivity to be carried away captive by delivering them up to Edom]* (Amos 1:6).

D. "They wanted to flee to the east, but they did not let them: *Thus says the Lord, for three transgressions of Damascus, yes for four, I will not reverse it* (Amos 1:3).

E. "They wanted to flee to the north, but they did not let them: *Thus says the Lord, for three transgressions of Tyre, yes for four, I will not reverse it* (Amos 1:21).

F. "They wanted to flee to the west, but they did not let them: *The burden upon Arabia* (Is. 21:13).

G. "Said to them the Holy One, blessed be He, 'Lo, you outraged them.'

H. "They said before Him, 'Lord of the ages, are you not the one who did it? *[All my enemies, when they heard of my calamity, rejoiced at what* you *had done].*'"

.3 A. They drew a parable. To what may the matter be compared?

B. To the case of a king who married a noble lady, and gave her instructions, saying to her: "Do not talk with your neighbors, and do not lend anything to them, and do not borrow anything from them."

C. One time she made him mad, so he drove her out and dismissed her from his palace, and she made the rounds of the households of her neighbors, but there was not a single one who would accept her.

D. The king said to her, "Lo, you outraged them."

E. She said to him, "My lord, king, are you not the one who did it? Did you not give me instructions, say to me, 'Do not talk with your neighbors, and do not lend anything to them, and do not borrow anything from them.' If I had borrowed something from them or had lent something to them, which one of them would have seen me pass through her household and not accept me in her home?"

F. That illustrates the verse: *[All my enemies, when they heard of my calamity, rejoiced] at what* you *had done.*

G. Said Israel before the Holy One, blessed be He, "Lord of the ages, are you not the one who did this: Did you not write for us in the Torah: *You shall not make marriages with them: your daughter you shall not give to his son, nor his daughter shall you take for your son* (Deut. 7:3).

H. "If we had taken children in marriage from them, or given children in marriage to them, which one of them would have seen a son or daughter standing in trouble and not receive him?

I. That illustrates the verse: *[All my enemies, when they heard of my calamity, rejoiced[] at what* you *had done.*

.4 A.   *...but hasten the day you have promised when they shall become like me* (Lam. 2:21):

B.   Like me in sorrow, not like me in prosperity.

.5 A.   *...with no one to comfort me:*

B.   Said the Holy One, blessed be He, *I, even I, am He Who comforts you [who are you that you are afraid of a man who dies, of the son of man who is made like grass, and have forgotten the Lord, your Maker, who stretched out the heavens and laid the foundations of the earth, and fear continually all the day because of the fury of the oppressor, when he sets himself to destroy? And where is the fury of the oppressor? He who is bowed down shall speedily be released; he shall die and go down to the Pit, neither shall his bread fail. For I am the Lord your God, who stirs up the sea so that its waves roar – the Lord of hosts is his name]* (Isaiah 51:12-15).

The cited verse is applied to three cases, with the third one leading us directly to our base-verse. First we speak of Aaron, or, rather, of Israel at the time that Aaron died. This application seems to me not very rich, since all we have is a reference to one clause of the intersecting-verse, the rejoicing of enemies at what God had done. No. 2, by contrast, confronts each of the clauses, making the point that it is God who caused the entire catastrophe, specifically, Israel's loyalty to God's commandments. No. 3's parable restates in general terms what No. 2 has told us in very particular ones. Then the parable is applied to make the point that No. 2 has made. Nos. 4, 5 then bring the whole to the point at which we started, our base-verse, which has God comfort Israel, now having accepted the accusation that he also has brought the trouble on their head.

XIX:III

.1 A.   *As a father has compassion on his children so has the Lord compassion [on all who fear him. For he knows how we were made, how knows full well that we are dust]* (Ps. 103:13-14):

B.   Like which father?

C.   R. Hiyya taught on Tannaite authority: "Like the most merciful among the patriarchs."

D.   And who is the most merciful among the patriarchs?

E.   R. Azariah in the name of R. Aha, "This is our father Abraham.

F.   "You find that before the Holy One, blessed be He, brought the flood on the Sodomites, our father Abraham said before the Holy One, blessed be He, 'Lord of the ages, You have bound yourself by an oath not to bring a flood upon the world. What verse of Scripture indicates it? *These days recall for me the days of Noah, as I swore [that the waters of Noah's flood should never again pour over the earth, so now I swear to you never again to be angry with you or reproach you]* (Is. 54:9). True enough, you are not going to bring a flood of water, but you are going to bring a flood of fire. Are you now going to act deceitfully against the clear intent of that oath? [If so you will not carry out the oath!]

G.   "*'Far be it from you to do this thing, [to kill the righteous like the wicked]* (Gen. 18:25).'"

H.   Said R. Levi, '*Will not the judge of all the earth do justly?* (Gen. 18:25). If justice is what you want, there can be no world, and if you want to have a world, there can be no justice. Why do you hold the rope at both ends? You want your world and you want justice. If you don't give in a bit, the world can never stand.'"

.2 A.   R. Joshua bar Nehemiah interpreted the verse to speak of our father, Jacob:

B.   "*And he himself went on before them and he bowed down* (Gen. 33:3):

C.   "What is the meaning of the statement, *and he?*

D.   "He was still in distress. He said, 'It is better that he lay hands on me and not on my children.'

E.   "What did he do? He armed them, and then dressed them in white garments on the outside and prepared himself for three matters: to say a prayer, to give a gift, and to fight a battle.

F.   "...to say a prayer: *Save me, I pray you, from the hand of my brother* (Gen. 32:2).

G.   "...to give a gift: *And the gift passed before him* (Gen. 32:22).

H.   "...and to fight a battle: *And he said, If Esau comes to the one camp and smites it* (Gen. 32:9).

I.   "'From this point onward, we shall have a battle with him.'"

.3 A.   Said R. Samuel, "It is the way of the father to have compassion: *As a father has compassion on children* (Ps. 103:13).

B.   "It is the way of the mother to comfort: *Like a man whose mother comforts him* (Is. 66:13).

C.   "Said the Holy One, blessed be He, 'I shall do the part of the father, I shall do the part of the mother.'

D.   "'I shall do the part of the father: *As a father has compassion on children* (Ps. 103:13).

E.   "'I shall do the part of the mother: *Like a man whose mother comforts him* (Is. 66:13).

F.   "'Said the Holy One, blessed be He, *I, even I, am he who comforts you [who are you that you are afraid of a man who dies, of the son of man who is made like grass, and have forgotten the Lord,*

your Maker, who stretched out the heavens and laid the
foundations of the earth, and fear continually all the day because
of the fury of the oppressor, when he sets himself to destroy?
And where is the fury of the oppressor? He who is bowed down
shall speedily be released; he shall die and go down to the Pit,
neither shall his bread fail. For I am the Lord your God, who
stirs up the sea so that its waves roar – the Lord of hosts is his
name] (Isaiah 51:12-15).'"

The intersecting-verse proves entirely congruent to the task of illuminating the base-verse, and the message of God's personal role in comforting Israel is stated with great emotional power by introducing the parallel of the mercy of the patriarchs, on the one side, Nos. 1, 2, and then of the natural father and mother, on the other, No. 3. God does the work of both father and mother, leading us to the base-verse which underlines that it is God personally who brings comfort.

XIX:IV

.1 A.   R. Abba bar Kahana in the name of R. Yohanan: "The matter may be compared to the case of a king who betrothed a noble lady and wrote for her in the marriage settlement a sizable pledge: 'So and so many marriage canopies I shall prepare for you, such and so ornaments I shall provide for you, so and so many treasurers I shall give you.'

B.   "He then left her and went overseas, and she waited there for many years. Her friends were making fun of her, saying, 'How long are you going to sit? Get yourself a husband while you are still young, while you are still vigorous.'

C.   "And she would go into her house and take the document of her marriage-settlement and read it and find comfort. After some time the king came home from overseas. He said to her, 'My daughter, I am amazed at how you have had faith in me all these years.'

D.   "She said to him, 'My lord, king, were it not for the substantial marriage settlement that you wrote out for me, my friends would have made you lose me.'

E.   "So too, since in this world, the nations of the world ridicule Israel, saying to them, 'How long are you going to be put to death for the sake of your God and give your lives for him and be put to death for him? How much pain does he bring on you, how much humiliation he brings on you, how much pain he brings on you. Come to us and we shall appoint you commanders and governoers and generals.'

F.   "Then the Israelites enter their meeting places and study halls and take the scroll of the Torah and read in it: *And I shall walk in your midst, and I shall make you prosper, and I shall make you numerous, and I shall carry out my covenant with you* (Lev. 26:9).

G.   "When the end will come, the Holy One, blessed be He, will say to Israel, 'I am amazed at how you have had faith in me all these years.'

H.   "And Israel will say before the Holy One, blessed be He, 'Lord of the ages, were it not for the scroll of the Torah which you wrote out for us, the nations of the world would have succeeded in destroying us for you.

I.   "That is in line with this verse of Scripture: *I recall to mind therefore I have hope* (Lam. 3:21).

J.   "And so too David says, *Unless your Torah had been my delight, I should then have perished in my affliction* (Ps. 119:92)."

I cannot imagine a more powerful statement, but why it serves our pisqa I cannot say, since it is at best thematically relevant. But it ignores the work at hand. The parable states in general terms what the exegesis proceeds to spell out in particular ones. My best sense is that the composition has been worked out in its own terms and then selected for use here because of its obvious thematic pertinence.

XIX:V

.1 A.   Another interpretation of the verse, *I, even I, am he who comforts you [who are you that you are afraid of a man who dies, of the son of man who is made like grass, and have forgotten the Lord, your Maker, who stretched out the heavens and laid the foundations of the earth, and fear continually all the day because of the fury of the oppressor, when he sets himself to destroy? And where is the fury of the oppressor? He who is bowed down shall speedily be released; he shall die and go down to the Pit, neither shall his bread fail. For I am the Lord your God, who stirs up the sea so that its waves roar – the Lord of hosts is his name]* (Isaiah 51:12-15)

B.   R. Abun in the name of R. Simeon b. Laqish: "The matter may be compared to the case of a king who grew angry with his noble wife and drove her out and put her away from his palace. After some time he wanted to bring her back. She said, 'Let him double the sum promised in my marriage settlement and then he can bring me back.'

C.   "So too [in the case of Israel] thus said the Holy One, blessed be He, to Israel, 'My children, at Sinai I said to you one time, I am the Lord your God (Ex. 20:2), but in Jerusalem in the coming age I shall say it to you two times: *I, even I, am he who comforts you.'*

.2 A.   R. Menahamah in the name of R. Abin, "[God said,] 'Of that very consolation that you laid before me at Mount Sinai, when you said, *All that the Lord has spoken we shall do and we shall hear* (Ex. 24:7), [you are assured of comfort]. *Why are you afraid* (Is. 51:12).

B.   "'Are you not the one who said to me at the sea, *Who is like you* (Ex. 15:11)? *Who are you that you are afraid of a man who dies, of the son of man who is made like grass?'*"

.3 A.   R. Berekhiah in the name of R. Helbo, R. Samuel bar Nahman in the name of R. Jonathan: "The Israelites were worthy of being annihilated in the time of Haman. But they relied on the judgment of the elder and said, 'If our father, Jacob, whom the Holy One, blessed be He, promised, saying to him, *Lo, I shall be with you and guard you wherever you go* (Gen. 28:15), yet he feared, we how much the more so should fear!'

B.   "That is why the prophet rebukes them, saying to them, *'...have forgotten the Lord, your Maker, who stretched out the heavens and laid the foundations of the earth?*

C.   "'Have you forgotten what I said to you, *If heaven is measured and the foundations of the earth search out beneath, then will I cast off all the seed of Israel for all that they have done, says the Lord* (Jer. 31:37).

D.   "'Have you seen heaven measured or the foundations of the earth searched out?

E.   "'From the stretching out of the heavens and the laying of the foundations of the earth you should have learned. But rather, *you fear continually all the day because of the fury of the oppressor, when he sets himself to destroy? [And where is the fury of the oppressor? He who is bowed down shall speedily be released; he shall die and go down to the Pit, neither shall his bread fail. For I am the Lord your God, who stirs up the sea so that its waves roar – the Lord of hosts is his name]* (Isaiah 51:12-15).'"

.4 A.   Said R. Isaac, "[The reason that *you fear continually all the day because of the fury of the oppressor]* is that troubles follow in close succession."

.5 A.   *And where is the fury of the oppressor?*
B.   That is Haman and his party.
C.   *...when he sets himself to destroy:* (Isaiah 51:13) *in the first month, that is the month of Nisan* (Est. 3:7).

.6 A.   *He who is bowed down shall speedily be released; he shall not die and go down to the Pit:*

B.   Said R. Abbahu, "There are six things that are a good sign for one who is sick: sneezing, sweating, sleeping, a nocturnal emission, dreaming, and regular bowel movements:

C.   "sneezing: *His sneezings flash forth light* (Job 41:10);

D.   "sweating: *In the sweat of your face you shall eat bread* (Gen. 3:19);

E.   "a nocturnal emission: *Seeing seed, he shall prolong his days* (Is. 53:10);

F.   "sleeping: *I should have slept, then I would have been at ease* (Job 3:13);

G.   "dreaming: *You caused me to dream and made me live* (Is. 38:16);

H.   "and regular bowel movements: *He who is bowed down shall speedily be released; he shall not die and go down to the Pit;"*

I.   Said R. Haggai, "And that is on condition that he should not lack for bread [but eats regularly]."

We proceed to the phrase-by-phrase exegesis of our base-verse. No. 1 once more lights on the doubling, *I even I*. This is given a strong application. Nos. 2, 3 yield some textual problems, though I believe I have stated the gist of the matter accurately. No. 3 clearly wishes to read one clause in the light of another. No. 4 seems another fragment. No. 5 also does not appear to be fully spelled out. No. 6 presents a syllogism independent of our setting, to which our base-verse contributes a proof-text.

XIX:VI

.1 A.   *For I am the Lord your God, who stirs up the sea so that its waves roar – the Lord of hosts is his name]* (Isaiah 51:12-15):

B.   And why did the sea flee?

C.   R. Judah and R. Nehemiah:

D.   R. Judah said, "It was the staff of Moses that the sea saw and from which it fled."

E.   R. Nehemiah said, "It was the Ineffable Name that was incised on it: *the Lord of hosts is his name,* that the sea saw and on account of which it fled."

.2 A.   *I have put my words in your mouth and have covered you in the shadow of my hand [that I may plant the heavens and lay the foundations of the earth]* (Is. 51:16):

B.   There we have learned in a passage of the Mishnah: **Simeon the righteous was one of the last of the remnants of the Great Assembly. [He would say, "On three things the world**

endures: **Torah, deeds of lovingkindness, and the Temple service"**] (Fathers 1:2).

.3 A.   R. Huna in the name of R. Aha: "Those who passed through the sea explained the matter: *You in your kindness have led the people which you have redeemed* (Ex. 15:13).

B.   "This refers to acts of loving kindness.

C.   *"You have guided them in your strength* (Ex. 15:14).

D.   "This refers to the Torah.

E.   *"When the Lord gave strength to his people, he blessed them with peace* (Ps. 29:11).

F.   "Yet the world still trembles. When will the world be set on a secure foundation?

G.   "When *they come to your holy habitation* (Ex. 15:14) [that is to say, the Temple, the third item in Simeon's list]."

.4 A.   There we have learned: **Rabban Simeon ben Gamaliel says, "The world is established on three things...And all of them derive from a single verse of Scripture: *These are the things you shall do: speak every man the truth to his neighbor, do justice and make peace in your gates* (Zech. 8:16)."**

B.   And all three of them are one thing: If justice is done, then truth is carried out and peace is made.

.5 A.   R. Joshua of Sikhnin in the name of R. Levi: *"I have put my words in your mouth [and have covered you in the shadow of my hand that I may plant the heavens and lay the foundations of the earth]* (Isaiah 51:16):

B.   *"I have put my words in your mouth:* this refers to words of Torah.

C.   *"...and have covered you in the shadow of my hand:* this refers to acts of loving kindness.

D.   "This serves to teach you that whoever is occupied with study of the Torah and with acts of loving kindness gains the merit of taking refuge in the shadow of the Holy One, blessed be He."

E.   "That is in line with this verse of Scripture: *How precious is your loving kindness which you commanded, because of it men take refuge in the shadow of your wings* (Ps. 36:8).

F.   *"...that I may plant the heavens and lay the foundations of the earth:* this refers to the offerings."

G.   *And say to Zion, you are my people*:

H.   Said R. Hanina bar Papa, "We have made the rounds of the whole of Scripture and have never found another passage in which Israel is called Zion.

I.   "But where is there such a passage? *And say to Zion, you are my people.*"

The exegesis of the concluding clause of the base-verse is somewhat disjoined, since No. 1 does not serve our passage, but merely draws upon it as a proof-text for its own purpose. No. 2 has in mind to link our concluding phrase to the matter of Toprah, deeds of lovingkindness, and the sacrificial cult, and this exposition does succeed, though it too is not without its imperfections. No. 3 interrupts the exposition, for one thing. No. 4 is irrelevant. But at No. 5 we have a most successful exercise, and a suitable conclusion to the whole.

VII

Sing aloud, O barren woman who never bore a child, break into cries of joy, you who have never been in labor; for the deserted wife has more sons than she who lives in wedlock, says the Lord. Enlarge the limits of your home, spread wide the curtains of your tent; let out its ropes to the full and drive the pegs home; for you shall break out of your confines right and left, your descendants shall dispossess wide regions and repeople cities now desolate. Fear not; you shall not be put to shame, you shall suffer no insult, have no cause to blush. It is time to forget the shame of your younger days and remember no more the reproach of your widowhood; for your husband is your maker, whose name is the Lord of hosts; your redeemer is the Holy One of Israel who is called God of all the earth. The Lord has acknowledged you a wife again, once deserted and heartbroken, your God has called you a bride

still young though once rejected. On the impulse of a moment I forsook you, but with tender affection I will bring you home again. In sudden anger I hid my face from you for a moment; but now have I pitied you with a love which never fails, says the Lord who ransoms you.
(Is. 54:1-8)

Pesiqta de Rab Kahana
Pisqa Twenty

XX:I

.1 A.   *...who makes the woman in a childless house a happy mother of children* (Ps. 113:9):

B.   There are seven childless women [in Scripture]: Sarah, Rebecca, Rachel, Leah, the wife of Manoah, Hannah, and Zion.

.2 A.   Another interpretation of the verse *...who makes the woman in a childless house a happy mother of children* (Ps. 113:9):

B.   This refers to our mother, Sarah: *And Sarah was barren* (Gen. 11:30).

C.   *As a joyful mother of children* (Ps. 113:9): *Sarah has given children suck* (Gen. 21:7).

.3 A.   Another interpretation of the verse *...who makes the woman in a childless house a happy mother of children* (Ps. 113:9):

B.   This refers to our Rebecca: *And Isaac entreated to the Lord on account of his wife, because she was barren* (Gen. 25:21).

C.   *As a joyful mother of children* (Ps. 113:9): *And the Lord was entreated by him and his wife Rebecca conceived* (Gen. 25:21).

.4 A.   Another interpretation of the verse *...who makes the woman in a childless house a happy mother of children* (Ps. 113:9):

B.   This refers to Leah: *And the Lord saw that Leah was hated and he opened her womb* (Gen. 29:31). On the basis of that statement we learn that Leah had been barren.

C.   *As a joyful mother of children* (Ps. 113:9): *For I have born him six sons* (Gen. 30:20).

.5 A.   Another interpretation of the verse ...*who makes the woman in a childless house a happy mother of children* (Ps. 113:9):

B.   This refers to Rachel: *And Rachel was barren* (Gen. 29:31).

C.   *As a joyful mother of children* (Ps. 113:9): *The children of Rachel: Joseph and Benjamin* (Gen. 35:24).

.6 A.   Another interpretation of the verse ...*who makes the woman in a childless house a happy mother of children* (Ps. 113:9):

B.   This refers to the wife of Manoah: *And the angel of the Lord looked at the woman and said to her, Lo, you are barren and have not born children* (Judges 13:3).

C.   *As a joyful mother of children* (Ps. 113:9): *And you will conceive and bear a son* (Judges 13:3).

.7 A.   Another interpretation of the verse ...*who makes the woman in a childless house a happy mother of children* (Ps. 113:9):

B.   This refers to the Hannah: *And Peninah had children but Hannah had no children* (1 Sam. 1:2).

C.   *As a joyful mother of children* (Ps. 113:9): *And she conceived and bore three sons and two daughters* (1 Sam. 2:21).

.8 A.   Another interpretation of the verse ...*who makes the woman in a childless house a happy mother of children* (Ps. 113:9):

B.   This refers to Zion: *Sing aloud, O barren woman [who never bore a child, break into cries of joy, you who have never been in labor; for the deserted wife has more sons than she who lives in wedlock, says the Lord. Enlarge the limits of your home, spread wide the curtains of your tent; let out its ropes to the full and drive the pegs home; for you shall break out of your confines right and left, your descendants shall dispossess wide regions and repeople cities now desolate. Fear not; you shall not be put to shame, you shall suffer no insult, have no cause to blush. It is time to forget the shame of your younger days and remember no more the reproach of your widowhood; for your husband is your maker, whose name is the Lord of hosts; your redeemer is the Holy One of Israel who is called God of all the earth. The Lord has acknowledged you a wife again, once deserted and heartbroken, your God has called you a bride still young though once rejected. On the impulse of a moment I forsook you, but with tender affection I will bring you home again. In sudden anger I hid my face from you for a moment; but now have I pitied you with a love which never fails, says the Lord who ransoms you]* (Is. 54:1-8).

The catalogue generated by the base-verse accomplishes the goal of comparing Zion to the barren women who ultimately bore important children. The pertinence of the intersecting-verse to the base-verse cannot be called into question, and the result is a powerful statement of the context of the base-verse and therefore of its meaning.

XX:II

.1 A.   Said R. Reuben, "The meaning of the words, *Sing aloud, O barren woman*, [Mandelbaum: the letters of "O" may be read as though they sounded out the words, *become pregnant*]."

.2 A.   Said R. Meir, "The letters of the word for *barren women* may be read to mean *uprooted woman*. It is a nation that the nations of the world have uprooted.

    B.   "That is in line with this verse of Scripture: *Remember, O Lord, against the children of Edom, the day of Jerusalem the day they said, raze it, raze it* (Ps. 137:7):

    C.   R. Abba bar Kahana said, "The meaning of the Hebrew word translated *raze it* follows the sense of the same word as it occurs in the following verse: *The broad walls of Babylon shall be utterly razed* (Jer. 51:58)." [Giving the remainder as already presented above, **XVIII:II**: R. Levi said, "The meaning of the Hebrew word translated *raze* it should be rendered as *empty it, empty it*, for it follows the sense of the same word as it occurs in the following verse: *She hastened and emptied her pitcher into the trough* (Gen. 24:20)." In the view of R. Abba bar Kahana, who holds that the word means *raze it, raze it*, the sense is that they went down to the very foundations, to the base. In the view of R. Levi, who holds that the word means, *empty it out, empty it out,* the sense is that they cut away the foundations, taking them away.]

.3 A.   Said R. Abba bar Kahana, "[With reference to the verse, *The Lord make you...like Rachel and like Leah* (Ruth 4:11), the blessing said by the guests at Boaz's wedding to Ruth], most of those assembled were of the side of Leah but they mentioned the name of Rachel first, as you say, *And Rachel was barren* (Gen. 29:31)."

    B.   Said R. Isaac, "[Reading the letters of the word *barren* to sound the word *the principal*,] it is because Rachel was the principal of the household, as you say, *And Rachel was barren* (Gen. 29:31)."

    C.   It was taught on Tannaite authority in the name of R. Simeon b. Yohai, "It is because everything depended on Rachel, therefore all of the children were called in her name: *Rachel is weeping for her children* (Jer. 31:14).

D. "And it is not the end of the matter that they are called in her name, but even in the name of her son: *Perhaps the Lord of hosts will show favor to the remnant of Joseph* (Amos 5:15).

E. "And even in the name of the son of her son: *Is not Ephraim my favorite son* (Jer. 31:19). [All of these verses intend to speak of the whole of Israel.]"

We shift to a different exegetical mode, namely, the phrase-by-phrase interpretation of the base-verse in its own terms. Once we have dealt with our verse, we take up the secondary accretion of the proof-text, already given above. The inclusion of No. 3 seems to me for essentially anthological reasons. Once we deal with Rachel and Leah, we proceed to collect pertinent materials on that theme.

XX:III

.1 A. *...who never bore a child:*

B. Said R. Levi, "In any passage in which it is said, 'She had no...,' she eventually would have. [The rest of the passage is as given above, **XVIII:III.1**: *And Sarai was barren, she had no child* (Gen. 11:30). *Will Sarah give suck to children* (Gen. 21:7). [Better: *And the Lord remembered Sarah* (Gen. 21:1)]. *And Peninah had children but Hannah had no children* (1 Sam. 1:2). *And the Lord visited Hannah and she conceived and she bore three sons* (1 Sam. 2:21). *She is Zion, there is none who cares for her* (Jer. 30:17). *And a redeemer will come to Zion and to those who turn from transgression* (Is. 59:20).]"

We have a citation of an earlier passage, now attached to a phrase of our base-verse.

XX:IV

.1 A. *... break into cries of joy, you who have never been in labor:*

B. There are ten words for rejoicing: [Braude and Kapstein, pp. 332-333:] gladness, merriment, joy, exulting, jubilation, shouting, a ringing cry, a shrill cry, a resounding cry, and a trumpet blast.

C. Some remove trumpet blast and substitute the word for leaping: *Before him leaps terror* (Job 41:14).

D. Leaping up like a flying fish [Mandelbaum].

The exegesis of the successive clauses continues.

XX:V

.1 A. *...for the deserted wife has more sons than she who lives in wedlock, says the Lord:*

B.   Said R. Abba bar Kahana, "It is written, *And your mouth is comely* [Braude and Kapstein, p. 333: *When the Dwelling is become thy desolation.* Note: *Thy mouth* can also mean *thy wilderness, thy desolation*; and *comely* is construed as though spelled as *residence, temple*] (Song 4:3).

C.   "Even though the habitation is turned into a wilderness, still, [unclean persons who entered into the Temple area] are liable for [contaminating] the space within its bounds though the building is destroyed, even as they are liable for violating its bounds when the Temple is built [and standing]."

D.   Said R. Levi, "When it was standing, it made a place for me for the wicked, such as Ahaz, Manasseh, and Amon. When it was destroyed, it made a place for me for righteous, such as Daniel and his allies, Mordecai and his allies, Ezra and his allies."

E.   R. Aha in the name of R. Yohanan: "It made a place for me for many more righteous ones when it was destroyed than it did when it was standing."

The clause of the base-verse cited at the outset is interpreted to mean that the Temple when destroyed marked an age of greater presence of the righteous than when it was standing. The mode of expressing the thought seems somewhat arcane because of the proof-text at hand, which Braude and Kapstein seem to me to have read as the original exegete intended.

XX:VI

.1 A.   *May there be abundance of grain in the land, growing in plenty to the tops of the hills; may the crops flourish like Lebanon, [and the sheaves be numberless as blades of grass. Long may the king's name endure, may it live forever like the sun; so shall all peoples pray to be blessed as he was, all nations tell of his happiness]* (Ps. 72:16-17):

B.   [With reference to *the tree of knowledge* (Gen. 2:9)]: What was the tree from which Adam and Eve ate?

C.   R. Meir says, "In fact it was wheat."

D.   R. Judah bar Ilai said, "It was grapes."

E.   R. Abba of Acre said, "It was the *etrog.*"

F.   R. Yose said, "It was figs."

G.   And all of them produced a reason [or a verse of Scripture] to back up their views:

H.   As to the reason for the position of R. Meir, who said, "In fact it was wheat," when someone has no knowledge, people say, "That man has never in his life eaten bread made out of wheat."

I. R. Zeora asked R. Samuel bar R. Isaac, "In that connection it is written that it was a tree, and you say that it was wheat?"

J. He said to him, "It came from date trees, which grew as tall as the cedars of Lebanon, and they would scatter their seed on the earth."

K. As to the reason of R. Judah bar Ilai, who said, "It was grapes that Adam and Eve ate," it is as it is said, *Their grapes are grapes of gall, they have clusters of bitterness* (Deut. 32:32). [Those were the grapes that brought bitterness into the world.]

L. As to the reason of R. Abba of Acre, who said, "It was the *etrog*," it is in line with this verse: *And she ate [the fruit] of the trees* (Gen. 3:6), that is a tree that produces wood that can be eaten just as much as its fruit can be eaten, and and what is it? It is only the *etrog*.

M. As to the reason for the view of R. Yose, who said, said, "It was figs," he adduces this verse: *And they sewed fig leaves and made loin cloths for themselves* (Gen. 3:7).

N. R. Joshua of Sikhnin in the name of R. Levi: "The matter may be compared to the case of a king who had a son, who had many slave girls. He commanded him, saying to him, 'My son, take care that you not lay a hand on any one of these slave girls.' What did he do? The prince misbehaved with one of his slave girls.

O. "When the king heard about it, he drove him out of the palace, and the prince went begging at the doors of slave girls, but not one of them would not accept him. But the one with whom he had misbehaved opened her door to him and accepted him.

P. "So at the moment at which the first man ate from that tree, [and God drove him out of the Garden of Eden, and man went begging among all the trees, but none would accept him. All of the trees were heard saying, 'Here comes the thief who deceived his creator, here comes the thief who deceived his master.'

Q. "[That is in line with the following verse of Scripture:] *Let not the foot of presumption come to me and let not the hand of the wicked shake me* (Ps. 36:12):

R. *"Let not the foot of presumption come to me* meaning, 'the foot that presumed against its creator' [Freedman, *Genesis Rabbah, ad loc.*],

S. *"...and let not the hand of the wicked shake me* (Ps. 36:12), meaning, 'do not let it take a leaf from me.'

T. "So it turns out that one must say: 'The very same tree that produced the fruit is the tree that produced the leaves: *And they sewed fig leaves and made loin cloths for themselves* (Gen. 3:7).'"

U.   And what sort of fig tree was it?

V.   R. Abin said, "It was a *bart sheba* fig, for it brought seven [*sheba*] days of mourning into the world."

W.   R. Berekhiah in the name of R. Simon in the name of R. Joshua b. Levi: "In point of fact the Holy One, blessed be He, did not reveal the name of that particular tree to man, and it is not destined to be revealed.

X.   "Said the Holy One, blessed be He, 'It is written, *[And if a woman approach any beast and lie down with it], you shall kill the woman and the beast* **(Lev. 20:16). Now if man has sinned, what sin did the beast commit, [that it should be put to death too]?**

Y.   "But it is because a disaster came to a human being on its account. Therefore, said the Holy One, blessed be He, 'Let it be stoned to death.'

Z.   "Another matter: **It is so that that beast should not walk about in the market place, while people say, 'It was because of that beast that so-and-so was stoned to death.'** Said the Holy One, blessed be He, **'Now if it is on account of the honor owing to [Adam's] descendants that God took account, on account of his own honor, how much the more so'** [M. San. 7:4]." [Freedman, *Genesis Rabbah*, p. 124, n. 6: Similarly, God did not reveal the nature of the tree that it might not be said,"Through this tree Adam brought death into the world."]

It have not got the slightest idea why the compositor of our pisqa has found useful this vast composition, borrowed from Gen. R. verbatim. But the reference to the fig tree, in the following pericope, may have led to the joining of the two enormous pericopae, though, if that is the case, it is an extreme even for the redactional principle of aggregation through thematic association.

XX:VII

.1 A.   [With reference to the clause, *Enlarge the limits of your home, spread wide the curtains of your tent; let out its ropes to the full and drive the pegs home; for you shall break out of your confines right and left, your descendants shall dispossess wide regions and repeople cities now desolate:]* there is this case: R. Eleazar b. Azariah and R. Eliezer the Modite were in session, dealing with the verse, *At that time they shall call Jerusalem the throne of the Lord* (Jer. 3:17).

B.   R. Eleazar ben Azariah said to R. Eleazar the Modite, "Could Jerusalem hold them all?"

C.   He said to him, "The Holy One, blessed be He, is destined to say to [the city], 'Get longer, get wider, and receive your people: *Enlarge the limits of your home, spread wide the curtains of your tent.*"

.2 A.   Said R. Yohanan, "Jerusalem is destined to reach to the gates of Damascus.

B.   "What verse of Scripture indicates it?

C.   "*The burden of the word of the Lord. In the land of Hadrak and in Damascus shall be his resting place* (Zech. 9:1)."

.3 A.   What is the meaning of *Hadrak*?

B.   R. Judah and R. Nehemiah:

C.   R. Judah said, "This word refers only to the king-messiah, who is sharp (*had*) with the nations of the world, and tender (*rakh*) with Israel."

D.   R. Nehemiah said, "It is the place itself which is called *Hadrak*."

E.   Said R. Yose b. Dormaskit, "By the Temple service! I personally come from Damascus, and there is a place there that is called *Hadrak*."

F.   He said to him, "And how then do you interpret the clause, *[In the land of Hadrak] and in Damascus shall be his resting place*?"

G.   [He said to him,] "Just as a fig is narrow at the bottom and broad at the top, so Jerusalem is destined to be made broad as it goes upward, and the exiles will come and take rest under it, so carrying out the verse: *and in Damascus shall be his resting place.*

H.   "And *resting place* refers only to Jerusalem, as it is said, *This is my resting place for ever, here will I dwell, for I have desired it* (Ps. 132:14)."

I.   He said to him, "And how do you interpret the clause, *And the city will be rebuilt on its own ruins* (Jer. 30:18)?"

J.   He said to him, "For it is not destined to move from its spot, but it will be made broad on all sides as it goes upward, and the exiles will come and take rest under it. This serves to carry out the verse of Scripture: *for you shall break out of your confines right and left.* (Isaiah 54:3)"

.4 A.   So much for the length. How do we know that that is the case for the breadth? *From the tower of Hananel to the king's hollows* (Zech. 14:10).

B.   R. Berekhiah said, "To the ocean."

C.   R. Zakkai the Elder said, "To the shore of Jaffa."

D.   But they do not differ. The one who says it means, "To the ocean," maintains that the reference to *hollows* is to those that the King of kings of kings, blessed be He, will hollow out.

E.   The one who says it means, "To the shore of Jaffa," maintains that the reference to *hollows* is to those that Solomon hollowed out.

.5 A. So much for length and breadth. How do we know that that is the case for the height?

B.   *And there was an enlarging and a winding about still upward on the sides thereof* (Ez. 41:7).

.6 A. It was taught on Tannaite authority by R. Eleazar b. Jacob, "Jerusalem is destined to continued rising until it reaches the throne of glory, saying to the Holy One, blessed be He, *The place is too narrow for me, give a place where I may sit* (Is. 49:20).

.7 A. Yose b. R. Jeremiah, Dosetai in the name of R. Levi, "And still you do not know the true glory of Jerusalem. But it is written: *For I, says the Lord, will be to her a wall of fire round about and I will be the glory in the midst of her* (Zech. 2:9).

B.   "On the basis of that statement you know the true glory of Jerusalem."

No. 1 amplifies the reference in the base-verse, *Enlarge the limits of your home*. No. 2 forms a secondary amplification of that same matter. No. 3 carries forward No. 2. No. 4, 5, 6 then assume that we have had a reference to the length, then the breadth and height of Jerusalem. My sense is that the compositor wishes to carry forward 1.C: "Get longer, get wider." So he systematically inserts materials on the topic of the length, breadth, and then height of Jerusalem. It would have been satisfying had No. 7 brought us back to our base-verse, but, so far as I can see, the present pisqa is not among the more successful of the lot.

VIII

Arise, shine, [for your light has come, and the glory of the Lord has risen upon you. For behold, darkness shall cover the earth, and thick darkness the peoples; but the Lord will arise upon you and his glory will be seen upon you. And nations shall come to your light, and kings to the brightness of your rising]
(Isaiah 60:1-3)

Pesiqta deRab Kahana
Pisqa Twenty-One

XXI:I

.1 A.   *Therefore let the Lord be glorified in the regions of the east, [and the name of the Lord the God of Israel in the coasts and islands of the west]* (Is. 24:15):

B.   [Interpreting the word for regions of the east in its literal sense, lights:] with what do people honor him?

C.   With lights.

D.   R. Abbahu said, "With two lights: *And God made the two great lights* (Gen. 1:16).

E.   "How so? When the sun shines, people recite a blessing over it. When the moon comes out, people make a blessing over it."

F.   And rabbis say, "Said the Holy One, blessed be He, to Israel, 'My children, since my light is your light and your light is my light, let us – both you and I – together go and give light to Zion:

G.   *"'Arise, shine, [for your light has come, and the glory of the Lord has risen upon you. For behold, darkness shall cover the earth, and thick darkness the peoples; but the Lord will arise upon you and his glory will be seen upon you. And nations shall come to your light, and kings to the brightness of your rising]* (Isaiah 60:1-3).'"

The intersecting-verse leads in a straight line to the base-verse, now underlining the notion that both God and Israel bring light back to Zion.

XXI:II

.1 A.   R. Aha opened discourse by citing this verse, *"I am the Lord, that is my name* (Is. 42:8):

B.   "[God says,] 'That is the name that the first Man gave to me, that is the name for which I stipulated to myself, that is the name for which I stipulated with the ministering angels.'"

.2 A.   *I will not give my glory to another god, [nor my praise to any idol]* (Is. 42:8):

B.   R. Menahama in the name of R. Abin, "This refers to the *seirim* [referred to at Lev. 17:7 (Mandelbaum)]."

.3 A.   *...nor my praise to any idol:*

B.   Said the Holy One, blessed be He, "My glory I shall not give to another, but you give my praise to idols!

C.   "To whom shall I give it? To Zion:

D.   *"'Arise, shine, [for your light has come, and the glory of the Lord has risen upon you. For behold, darkness shall cover the earth, and thick darkness the peoples; but the Lord will arise upon you and his glory will be seen upon you. And nations shall come to your light, and kings to the brightness of your rising]* (Isaiah 60:1-3).'"

The systematic reading of the intersecting-verse produces the notion that God gives glory to Zion even while the Israelites assign it to things of this world.

XXI:III

.1 A.   *For with you is the fountain of life, in your light we see [New English Bible: are bathed with] light* (Ps. 36:10):

B.   R. Yohanan and R. Simeon b. Laqish:

C.   R. Yohanan made one statement, and R. Simeon b. Laqish two.

D.   R. Yohanan made one statement: "The matter may be compared to the case of someone who was walking along the way at dusk. Someone came and lit a light for him, which went out. Another one came and lit a light for him, which went out. He said, 'From this point on, I shall look forward only for the light of dawn.'

E.   "So said the Israelites to the Holy One, blessed be He, 'Lord of the ages, We made a lamp for you in the time of Moses, and it went out. We made ten in the time of Solomon, and they went out. From this time forth, we shall await only your light:

F.   "'...*in your light [alone] we see light* (Ps. 36:10).'"

.2 A.   R. Simeon b. Laqish made two statements:

B.   R. Simeon b. Laqish said, "The matter may be compared to the case of a king who had a since, and who invited guests to his [palace]. He said to his son, 'My son, do you want to eat with the guests?'

C.   "He said to him, 'No.'

D.   "He said to him, 'With whom do you wish to eat?'

E.   "He said to him, 'With you.'

F.   "So said the Holy One, blessed be He, 'My children, do you want to eat with the nations?'

G.   "They said before him, 'Lord of the ages, *Turn not my heart to sinful thoughts nor to any pursuit of evil courses. [The evildoers appal me, not for me the delights of their table. I would rather be battered by the rightous and reproved by good men]* (Ps. 141:4-5).'

H.   "He said to them, 'Is it because they pursue evil courses that you do not want to eat with them?'

I.   "They said before him, 'Lord of the ages, *not for me the delights of their table.* We really do not want even the good and handsome gifts of theirs, but what do we really want? We want the pleasant and handsome portions that come from you.'"

.3 A.   R. Simeon b. Laqish made yet another statement.

B.   R. Simeon b. Laqish said, "The matter may be compared to the case of a king who had a daughter, and someone came and asked for her in marriage, but he was not suitable for her. Then another came and asked for her in marriage, but he was not suitable for her. When yet a third came, who was suitable for her, and asked for her hand in marriage, he said, 'Arise, give light, for your light has come.'

C.   Said the Holy One, blessed be He, to Israel, 'My children, since my light is your light and your light is my light, let us – both you and I – together go and give light to Zion:

G.　　"'*Arise, shine, [for your light has come, and the glory of the Lord has risen upon you. For behold, darkness shall cover the earth, and thick darkness the peoples; but the Lord will arise upon you and his glory will be seen upon you. And nations shall come to your light, and kings to the brightness of your rising]* (Isaiah 60:1-3).'"

No. 1 gives us Yohanan's reading of the intersecting-verse entirely in its own terms. The passage then has been selected for use here only after formation around a different point of interest entirely. The composition thus serves our base-verse only incidentally, since the focus of discourse centers upon the intersecting-verse. But the compositor has so put things together as to leave us, at the end, with a powerful message deriving from our base-verse.

XXI:IV

.1 A.　　R. Phineas in the name of R. Reuben said, "The Holy One, blessed be He, is going to bring Sinai, Tabor, and Carmel, and to build the house of the sanctuary on top of them.

B.　　"What verse of Scripture indicates it? *In days to come the mountain of the Lord's house shall be set over all other mountains, lifted high above the hills. [All the nations shall come streaming to it, and many peoples shall come and say, 'Come, let us climb up on to the mountain of the Lord, to the house of the God of Jacob, that he may teach us his ways, and we may walk in his paths']* (Is. 2:2-3)."

C.　　Said R. Homa, "And is that enough for you? [There is more to be seen in the cited verse, specifically:] the house of the sanctuary will recite a song, and the mountains will respond to it.

D.　　"What verse of Scripture indicates it? *[In days to come the mounatin of the Lord's house shall be set over all other mountains,] lifted high above the hills* (Mic. 4:1). The word for lifted high bears the meaning of raising up a song, in line with this verse of Scripture: *Kenaniah, officer of the Levites, was in charge of the music, because of his proficiency, [Berechiah and Elkanah were door keepers for the ark, while the priests...sounded trumpets before the ark of God]* (1 Chr. 15:22-23)."

.2 A.　　R. Hoshaiah in the name of R. Epes: "Jerusalem is going to set up a beacon [conjectural] for the nations of the world and they will walk in its light.

B.　　"What verse of Scripture indicates it? *And nations shall come to your light, [and kings to the brightness of your rising]* (Isaiah 60:1-3)."

.3 A.   Said R. Aha, "Israel is compared to the olive: *A leafy olive tree, fair with goodly fruit* (Jer. 11:16).

B.   "The Holy One, blessed be He, is compared to a lamp: *The lamp of God is the soul of man* (Prov. 20:27).

C.   "Just as it is the way to put oil into a lamp, and then the two of them give light together, so said the Holy One, blessed be He, to Israel, 'My children, since my light is your light and your light is my light, let us – both you and I – together go and give light to Zion:

D.   "'Arise, shine, [for your light has come, and the glory of the Lord has risen upon you. For behold, darkness shall cover the earth, and thick darkness the peoples; but the Lord will arise upon you and his glory will be seen upon you. And nations shall come to your light, and kings to the brightness of your rising] (Isaiah 60:1-3).'"*

No. 1-2 follow their own interests, and No. 3 brings us back to the base-verse. The pattern remains the same throughout: the introduction of our base-verse proves adventitious and contrived.

XXI:V

.1 A.   R. Hiyya taught on Tannaite authority, "At the beginning of the creation of the world the Holy One, blessed be He, foresaw that the Temple would be built, destroyed, and rebuilt.

B.   *"In the beginning God created the heaven and the earth* (Gen. 1:1) [refers to the Temple] when it was built, in line with the following verse: *That I may plant the heavens and lay the foundations of the earth and say to Zion, You are my people* (Is. 51:16).

C.   *"And the earth was unformed* – lo, this refers to the destruction, in line with this verse: *I saw the earth, and lo, it was unformed* (Jer. 4:23).

D.   *"And God said, Let there be light* – lo, it was built and well constructed in the age to come."

.2 A.   R. Samuel bar Nahman: "While in this age people go by day in the light of the sun and by night in the light of the moon, in the coming age, they will undertake to go only by the light of the sun by day, and not by the light of the moon by night.

B.   "What verse of Scripture indicates it? *The sun shall no longer be your light by day, nor the moon shine on you when evening falls; [the Lord shall be your everlasting light, your God shall be your glory. Never again shall your sun set, nor your moon withdraw her light; but the Lord shall be your everlasting light and the days of your mourning shall be ended]* (Is. 60:19-20).

C.   "By what light will they walk? By the light of the Holy One, blessed be He, in line with the passage: *the Lord shall be your everlasting light.*"

.3 A.   Said R. Haninah, "There were windows in the house of the sanctuary, from which light shown outward into the world.

B.   "That is in line with the following verse of Scripture: *He made for the house windows that were broad and narrow* (1 Kgs. 6:4).

C.   "They were transparent and opaque, narrow on the inside and broad on the outside, so as to draw the light outward into the world."

.4 A.   Said R. Levi, "Under ordinary circumstances when someone builds a palace, he makes the windows so that they are narrow on the outside and broad on the inside, so as to bring the light inside.

B.   "But the windows of the house of the sanctuary were not that way. Rather they were narrow on the inside and broad on the outside, so as to draw the light outward into the world."

.5 A.   R. Berekhian in the name of R. BVesallah: "It is written, *And there were windows round about in it [and in its vestibule like the windows of the others]* (Ez. 40:25).

B.   "It is not written, 'Like this window,' but rather, *like the windows of the others.* They were dim and opque opaque, narrow on the inside and broad on the outside, so as to draw the light outward into the world."

.6 A.   R. Simeon b. Yehosedeq sent and asked R. Samuel b. Nahman, "Since I have heard that you are a master of lore, [I ask you this question:] When did the light go forth into the world?"

B.   He said to him, "The Holy One, blessed be He, cloaked himself in it as in a white garment and illuminated the entire world from the splendor of his glory."

C.   He said this to him in a whisper [as if it were a teaching of dubious authority].

D.   He said to him, "That is, in point of fact, a well-known verse of Scripture: *Who covers yourself with light as with a garment* (Ps. 104:2), so why do you repeat this to me in a whisper?"

E.   He said to him, "Just as others told it to me in a whisper, so I repeat it to you in a whisper. And if it were not for the fact that R. Isaac had expounded the same matter in public, it would not be permitted to repeat it at all."

F.   Before that time what did people say?

G. Said R. Berekhiah, "From the place of the house of the sanctuary light went forth to the world.

H. "That is in line with the following verse of Scripture: *And behold, the glory of the God of Israel came from the east and the sound of his coming was like the sound of many waters, and the earth shone with his glory* (Ez. 43:2).

I. "The word *glory* refers only to the house of the sanctuary, in line with this verse: *You throne of glory on high from the beginning, you place of our sanctuary* (Jer. 17:12)."

This entire composition is parachuted down from Leviticus Rabbah 31:7. It has no bearing on our base-verse, though it is relevant in a general way to the theme at hand. I see not the slightest effort to link the passage to our base-verse.

XXI:VI

.1 A. *For behold darkness shall cover the earth, and thick darkness the peoples; but the Lord will arise upon you, and his glory will be seen upon you. And nations shall come to your light, and kings to the brightness of your rising* (Is. 60:2-3):

B. R. Levi bar Zechariah in the name of R. Berekhiah: *"Darkness and thick darkness* affected Egypt for three days. And the rest of the pericope is as given in the pisqa, And it came to pass at midnight [as follows: What verse of Scripture indicates it? *And there was darkness, thick darkness* (Ex. 10:22). But emptiness and void have never yet affected this world. But where [and when] will they come to pass? They will envelop the great city of Rome: *He will stretch over it the line of chaos and the plummet of emptiness* (Is. 34:11)." Rabbis say, "As to the nations of the world, who never accepted the Torah which was given in darkness, concerning them Scripture says, *For behold darkness shall cover the earth, and thick darkness the peoples...*But as to Israel, which accepted it in darkness, concerning them Scripture says, *...but the Lord will arise upon you, and his glory will be seen upon you."]*

The closing statement underlines the foregoing, the contrast between Israel's coming glory, because of its acceptance of the Torah, and the nations' humiliation.

IX

I will greatly rejoice in the Lord, my soul shall exult in my God; for he has clothed me with the garments of salvation, he has covered me with the robe of righteousness, as a bridegroom decks himself with a garland, and as a bride adorns herself with her jewels. For as the earth brings forth its shoots, and as a garden causes what is sown in it to spring up, so the Lord God will cause righteousness and praise to spring forth before all the nations.
(Isaiah 61:10-11)

Pesiqta de Rab Kahana
Pisqa Twenty-Two

XXII:I

.1 A.   It is written, *Will you not revive us again [that your people may rejoice in you? Show us your steadfast love, O Lord, and grant us your salvation]* (Ps. 85:6-7):

  B.   Said R. Aha, "May your people and your city rejoice in you."

.2 A.   *And Sarah said, God has made joy for me; everyone who hears will rejoice with me* (Gen. 21:6):

B.   R. Yudan, R. Simon, R. Hanin, R. Samuel bar R. Isaac: "If Reuben is happy, what difference does it make to Simeon? So too, if Sarah was remembered, what difference did it make to anyone else? For lo, our mother Sarah says, *everyone who hears will rejoice with me* (Gen. 21:6).

C.   "But this teaches that when our mother, Sarah, was remembered, with her many barren women were remembered, with her all the deaf had their ears opened, with her all the blind had their eyes opened, with her all those who had lost their senses regained their senses. So everyone was saying, 'Would that our mother, Sarah, might be visited a second time, so that we may be visited with her!'

D.   [Explaining the source common joy,] R. Berekhiah in the name of R. Levi said, "She added to the lights of the heavens. The word *making* ['God has made joy'] is used here and also in the following verse: *And God made the two lights* (Gen. 1:16). Just as the word making used elsewhere has the sense of giving light to the world, so the word making used here has the sense of giving light to the world."

E.   "The word 'making' ['God has made joy'] is used here and also in the following verse: *And he made a release [of taxes] to the provinces* (Est. 2:18).

F.   "Just as the word 'making' used there indicates that a gift had been given to the entire world, so the word 'making'; used there indicates that a gift had been given to the entire world."

.3 A.   R. Berekhiah in the name of R. Levi: "You find that when our mother, Sarah, gave birth to Isaac, all the nations of the world said, 'God forbid! It is not Sarah that has given birth to Isaac, but Hagar, handmaiden of Sarah, is the one who gave birth to him.'

B.   "What did the Holy One, blessed be He, do? He dried up the breasts of the nations of the world, and their noble matrons came and kissed the dirt at the feet of Sarah saying to her, 'Do a religious duty and give suck to our children.'

C.   "Our father, Abraham, said to her, 'This is not a time for modesty, but [now, go forth, and] sanctify the name of the Holy One, blessed be He, by sitting [in public] in the market place and there giving suck to children.'

D.   "That is in line with the verse: *Will Sarah give suck to children* (Gen. 21:7).

E.   "What is written is not, *to a child*, but, *to children*.

F.   "And is it not an argument a fortiori: if in the case of a mortal, to whom rejoicing comes, the person rejoices and gives joy to everyone, when the Holy One, blessed be He, comes to give joy to Jerusalem, all the more so!

G. *"I will greatly rejoice in the Lord, [my soul shall exult in my God; for he has clothed me with the garments of salvation, he has covered me with the robe of righteousness, as a bridegroom decks himself with a garland, and as a bride adorns herself with her jewels. For as the earth brings forth its shoots, and as a garden causes what is sown in it to spring up, so the Lord God will cause righteousness and praise to spring forth before all the nations]* (Isaiah 61:10-11)."

No. 1 alludes to the base-verse but does not cite it and does not contribute to the interpretation of its meaning. No. 2 leads us to the conclusion at No. 3, which makes its simple point that when Jerusalem rejoices, everyone will have reason to join in.

XXII:II

.1 A. *This is the day which the Lord has made; let us rejoice and be glad in it* (Ps. 118:24):

B. Said R. Abin, "But do we not know in what to rejoice, whether in the day or in the Holy One, blessed be He? But Solomon came along and explained, We shall rejoice in you: in you, in your Torah, in you, in your salvation."

.2 A. Said R. Isaac, "In you (BK) [the Hebrew letters of which bear the numerical value of twenty-two, hence:] – in the twenty-two letters which you have used in writing the Torah for us.

B. "The B has the value of two, and the K of twenty."

.3 A. For we have learned in the Mishnah:

B. **If one has married a woman and lived with her for ten years and not produced a child, he is not allowed to remain sterile [but must marry someone else]. If he has divorced her, he is permitted to marry another. The second is permitted to remain wed with her for ten years. If she had a miscarriage, one counts from the time of the miscarriage. The man bears the religious duty of engaging in procreation but the woman does not. R. Yohanan b. Beroqah says, "The religious duty pertains to them both, for it is said, *And God blessed them* (Gen. 1:28)" [M. Yeb. 15:6].**

.4 A. There was a case in Sidon of one who married a woman and remained with her for ten years while she did not give birth.

B. They came to R. Simeon b. Yohai to arrange for the divorce. He said to her, "Any thing which I have in my house take and now go, return to your father's household."

C. Said to them R. Simeon b. Yohai, "Just as when you got married, it was in eating and drinking, so you may not separate from one another without eating and drinking."

D. What did the woman do? She made a splendid meal and gave the husband too much to drink and then gave a sign to her slave girl and said to her, "Bring him to my father's house."

E. At midnight the man woke up. He said to them, "Where am I?"

F. She said to him, "Did you not say to me, 'Any thing which I have in my house, take and now go, return to your father's household.' And that is how it is: I have nothing more precious than you."

G. When R. Simeon b. Yohai heard this, he said a prayer for them, and they were visited [with a pregnancy].

H. The Holy One, blessed be He, visits barren women, and the righteous have the same power.

I. "And is it not an argument a fortiori: if in the case of a mortal, to whom rejoicing comes, the person rejoices and gives joy to everyone, when the Holy One, blessed be He, comes to give joy to Jerusalem, all the more so! And when Israel looks forward to the salvation of the Holy One, blessed be He, all the more so!

J. *"I will greatly rejoice in the Lord, [my soul shall exult in my God; for he has clothed me with the garments of salvation, he has covered me with the robe of righteousness, as a bridegroom decks himself with a garland, and as a bride adorns herself with her jewels. For as the earth brings forth its shoots, and as a garden causes what is sown in it to spring up, so the Lord God will cause righteousness and praise to spring forth before all the nations]* (Isaiah 61:10-11)."

The same stereotype conclusion is tacked on to another story, rather well chosen in context, this one on a sequence of barren women who find reason to rejoice. I see no point of entry at No. 1, except a rather general interest in the theme of rejoicing. No. 2 carries forward the opening element. No. 3 leads us into No. 4, which is the goal of the framer of the whole.

XXII:III

.1 A. The matter may be compared to the case of a noble lady, whose husband, sons, and sons-in-law went overseas. They told her, "Your sons are coming."

B. She said to them, "My daughters-in-law will rejoice."

C. "Here come your sons-in-law!"

D. "My daughters will rejoice."

E. When they said to her, "Here comes your husband," she said to them, "Now there is occasion for complete rejoicing."

F. So to, the former prophets say to Jerusalem, *"Your sons come from afar* (Is. 60:4)."

G. And she says to them, *"Let Mount Zion be glad* (Ps. 48:12)."

H. *"Your daughters are carried to you on uplifted arms* (Is. 60:4)."

I. *"Let the daughters of Judah rejoice* (Ps. 48:12)."

J. But when they say to her, *"Behold your king comes to you* (Zech. 9:9)," then she will say to him, "Now there is occasion for complete rejoicing."

K. *I will greatly rejoice in the Lord, [my soul shall exult in my God; for he has clothed me with the garments of salvation, he has covered me with the robe of righteousness, as a bridegroom decks himself with a garland, and as a bride adorns herself with her jewels. For as the earth brings forth its shoots, and as a garden causes what is sown in it to spring up, so the Lord God will cause righteousness and praise to spring forth before all the nations]* (Isaiah 61:10-11)

The parable serves in general terms to make the point restated in particular ones about Jerusalem's complete rejoicing only when God makes his appearance there. That reading of the base-verse now gives way to a fresh message.

XXII:IV

.1 A. The matter may be compared to the case of an orphan girl who was raised in a palace. When the time came for her to be married, they said to her, "Do you have [for a dowry] anything at all?"

B. She said to them, "I do indeed: I have an inheritance from my father and I have an inheritance from my grandfather."

C. So Israel has the merit left to them by Abraham, and they have the inheritance of our father Jacob:

D. *He has clothed me with garments of salvation* (Is. 61:10) on account of the merit left by our father, Jacob: *And the hides of the offspring of goats she wrapped on his hands* (Gen. 27:16).

E. *He has covered me with the robe of righteousness* (Is. 61:10) refers to the merit left by our father, Abraham: *I have known him [to the end that he may command his children...to do righteousness]* (Gen. 16:19).

F.   ...*as a bridegroom decks himself with a garland, [and as a bride adorns herself with her jewels]* (Isaiah 61:10-11):

G.   You find that when the Israelites stood at Mount Sinai, they bedecked themselves like a bride, opening one and closing another eye [as a sign of modesty (Mandelbaum), and that merit the Israelites bequeathed to their children as well].

The next stage in the unfolding of discourse, that is the exposition of the clauses of our base-verse leads to yet another parable. The parable now underlines the Israelites' merit in expecting God's renewed relationship with them, this time deriving from Abraham, Jacob, and the whole of Israel at Sinai. The formal character of the parable is familiar in our document: first the general statement of matters, then the specific restatement in terms of Israel in particular.

XXII:V

.1 A.   In ten passages the Israelites are referred to as a bride, six by Solomon, three by Isaiah, and one by Jeremiah:

B.   Six by Solomon: *Come with me from Lebanon, my bride* (Song 4:8), *you have ravished my heart, my sister, my bride* (Song 4:9), *how beautiful is your love, my sister, my bride* (Song 4:10), *your lips drip honey, my bride* (Song 4:11), *a locked garden is my sister, my bride* (Song 4:12), and *I am come into my garden, my sister my bride* (Song 5:1).

C.   Three by Isaiah: *You shall surely clothe you with them as with an ornament and gird yourself with them as a bride* (Is. 49:18), the present verse, *as a bridegroom decks himself with a garland, and as a bride adorns herself with her jewels* (Isaiah 61:10-11), and *As the bridegroom rejoices over the bride* (Is. 62:5).

D.   One by Jeremiah: *The voice of joy and the voice of gladness, the voice of the bridgegroom and the voice of the bride* (Jer. 33:11).

E.   Corresponding to the ten passages in which Israel is spoken of as a bride, there are ten places in Scripture in which the Holy One clothed himself in a garment appropriate to each occasion:

F.   On the day on which he created the world, the first garment which the Holy One, blessed be He, put on was one of glory and majesty: *You are clothed with glory and majesty* (Ps. 104:1).

G.   The second garment, one of power, which the Holy One, blessed be He, put on was to exact punishment for the generation of the flood: *the Lord reigns, he is clothed with power* (Ps. 93:1).

H.   The third garment, one of strength, which the Holy One, blessed be He, put on was to give the Torah to Israel: *the Lord is clothed, he has girded himself with strength* (Ps. 93:1).

I. The fourth garment, a white one, which the Holy One, blessed be He, put on was to exact punishment from the kingdom of Babylonia: *his raiment was as white snow* (Dan. 7:9).

J. The fifth garment, one of vengeance, which the Holy One, blessed be He, put on was to exact vengeance from the kingdom of Media: *He put on garments of vengeance for clothing and was clad with zeal as a cloak* (Is. 59:17). Lo, here we have two [vengeance, zeal].

K. The seventh garment, one of righteousness and vindication, which the Holy One, blessed be He, put on was to exact vengeance from the kingdom of Greece: *He put on righteousness as a coat of mail and a helmet of deliverance upon his head* (Is. 59:17). Here we have two more [coat of mail, helmet].

L. The ninth garment, one of red, which the Holy One, blessed be He, put on was to exact vengeance from the kingdom of Edom [playing on the letters that spell both Edom and red]: *Why is your apparel red* (Is. 63:2).

M. The tenth garment, one of glory, which the Holy One, blessed be He, put on was to exact vengeance from Gog and Mag: *This one that is the most glorious of his apparel* (Is. 63:1).

N. Said the community of Israel before the oly One, blessed be He, "Of all the garments you have none more beautiful than this, as it is said, *the most glorious of his apparel* (Is. 63:1)."

The composition has been worked out in its own terms and is inserted here only because of the appearance of our base-verse as a proof-text.

South Florida Studies in the History of Judaism

South Florida Academic Commentary Series

South Florida-Rochester-Saint Louis
Studies on Religion and the Social Order

South Florida International Studies in
Formative Christianity and Judaism